TH... ...OF

ISRAEL

ERROLL HULSE

HENRY E. WALTER LTD, 26 GRAFTON ROAD, WORTHING

First published 1968
Second edition, revised and enlarged, 1971
Third edition 1982

ISBN 0 854 79000 4

Henry E Walter, Ltd
26, Grafton Road,
Worthing, Sussex
Printed and bound in Great Britain at
The Camelot Press Ltd, Southampton

For I will
gather you out of all countries
and will bring you into your own land
Then will I sprinkle clean water upon you
and ye shall be clean
A new heart also
will I give you
Ez. 36: 24-26

God does sometimes enter into covenant with communities, as such. Thus he has covenanted with the whole human race that the world shall not be again destroyed by a deluge, and that the seasons shall continue to succeed each other, in regular order, until the end of time. Thus he covenanted with the Jews to be a God to them and to their seed for ever, and that they should be to him a people. This, it seems, is a perpetual covenant, which continues in force until the present day, and which renders certain the restoration of the Jews to the privileges of the church of God.   *Commentary on Romans,* page 381
Charles Hodge – leading systematic
theologian of the last century.

THE PURPOSE OF THIS BOOK

Major objectives:

1. To investigate Bible teaching concerning the spiritual restoration of the Jewish people.

2. To provide a thorough exposition of the crucial eleventh chapter of Paul's epistle to the Romans, and establish the fact beyond all doubt, that Paul really means the Jews when he says 'all Israel'.

3. To relate the latter to the contemporary position of the Jews today.

4. To quicken interest in winning the confidence of Jews in regard to the true Gospel.

Secondary objectives:

5. To introduce the whole subject of Israel to those whose interest has just begun.

6. To discuss elementary principles of prophetic interpretation.

7. To furnish an outline of the different prophetic views.

8. To outline the history of Jerusalem so that recent events may be judged in the light of that history.

9. To warn against the misuse of prophecy.

10. To supply an adequate bibliography for those who wish to study the subject of Israel in more detail.

PREFACE TO FIRST EDITION

The territorial restoration of the ancient land of Israel to the Jewish people and the consolidation of that country to the point where she is now the foremost nation of the Middle East, has involved a series of events which even non-religious people describe as miraculous.

The conviction that these events form the prelude to a much greater miracle – the conversion of the Jewish people to New Testament Christianity – has resulted in this book. That the Puritans (whom many have regarded as the greatest of all Biblical expositors) held the view I set forth has been advantageous. I have leaned heavily upon them and upon the writings of those who have followed in the Puritan tradition. But it has been through the exercise of expository preaching to a village congregation that the subject became alive to me personally. I began weekly expositions of Romans in January 1963 and after five years completed the epistle in December 1967. That series of studies really gave birth to part two, *Romans Eleven*, which forms the major section of this volume.

At the same time as we were studying Romans we were working through the Gospel of Luke at our mid-week services. We had reached Luke 13: 34–35 – 'Ye shall not see me, until the time come when ye shall say, Blessed is he that cometh in the name of the Lord' – when the astonishing events of the Six-day war took place; 5–10 June 1967. Subsequent to this I outlined the subject of 'Will Israel become Christian?' (consisting of the 106th and 107th expositions in our consecutive study of Luke) in two articles which appeared in the July and August issues of *The Christian's Pathway* magazine. The response indicated widespread interest which prompted further research. These are some of the factors which have led to the chapters which follow.

Throughout, unless otherwise stated, the Authorized Version (King James) of the Bible has been quoted. In line with the latter the small 'h' has been used for pronouns referring to Deity.

PREFACE TO SECOND EDITION

Favourable reviews of *The Restoration of Israel* have appeared in most of the well-known evangelical journals in Britain. I am thankful for the thoroughness of some of these and have sought in the appendices to this edition to answer questions that have been raised. Some deemed it imprudent to assume that the territorial restoration is an accomplished fact in view of the formidable enemies that surround Israel, not to mention the threat of Russia. What is to prevent an army from sweeping across the Judean hills like a tidal wave to end Jewish dreams like sand-castles on the seashore? The spiritual conversion of the Jewish people as a whole is predicted in the clearest terms in Romans eleven. But there is no mention of *the land* of Israel.

For every Jew in Israel there are three elsewhere. The territorial restoration of Israel is not strictly necessary for the expectation held forth in the eleventh of Romans. However, since the publication of the first edition I find no reason to rescind what I have said either about Jerusalem or the land. While admitting that the question of the land is secondary, I am unmoved in my belief that God, in his ordering of providence, would have our attention drawn to the existence and reality of 'His land' and ancient people. There is no more appropriate place for this but the land of Israel, which, from the time of Abraham, has been the principal stage upon which the drama of redemption has been enacted.

For me, Romans eleven is irrefutably plain. Many have laboured in vain to make it say other than what it plainly declares. I am happy to concede ground by way of interpretation in almost all other passages which seem to spell out the territorial or spiritual restoration of the Jews. But in regard to the main argument, that is Romans eleven, concerning the Jews, their relationship to the Gentiles, and their interaction upon each other in three distinct eras (which is what that chapter is all about) I concede nothing, no, not so much as an inch.

Hebrew friends have been very helpful in pointing out paragraphs which are likely to be misunderstood, particularly by readers in Israel. For instance, where I used the term 'Christianity' I am referring exclusively to evangelical, Bible-believing, spiritual Christianity and by 'Christian' I mean the born-again Christian (see appendix E).

For encouragement received from friends in several countries I record my sincere gratitude.

PREFACE TO THIRD EDITION

During June 1982 Israel invaded Lebanon with stunning speed and ferocity. The suffering inflicted on many civilians not directly involved with the conflict between the PLO and Syria on the one hand and Israel on the other, has brought widespread condemnation from the world. It has also resulted in a division of opinion among the Jews themselves.

In defence of Israel's actions, Premier Begin, in an interview on BBC Television, made reference to the holocaust, one third of the Hebrew people being destroyed. One evil, however appalling, does not provide warrant for another.

In this book I do not attempt to deal with the colossal moral problem of the displaced Palestinians or their cause. Their own record is far from angelic. Israel and the Gentile nations are not operating on a spiritual basis. Some peoples are more humane, restrained and compassionate, and are given more common grace than others. That is an important subject but it is not my purpose to analyse it in my book. I refer in documentary style only to the fact of the reoccupation of ancient Canaan by the blood descendants of Abraham and their repossession of Jerusalem.

CONTENTS

INTRODUCTION – THE MYSTERY OF ISRAEL

I

Without king, temple or sacrifice, the Jews remain, after nearly two thousand years, a people enveloped in an aura of destiny. Since the turn of this century a revival of Zionism has increased in momentum.[1] Starting with a trickle and ending with a river, the Jews have been gathered together into the land promised to Abraham and his seed. More and more, Israel has become the object of world attention. The recent Six-day war, 5–10 June 1967, served not only to consolidate Israel's position territorially and establish her as the most powerful nation in the Middle East, but this astonishing event also helped to revive Jewish unity and as never before focus the interest of all nations upon the land where Jesus was born.

At the centre of the drama of the Six-day war, reported as front page news throughout the world, was the restoration of Old Jerusalem to the Jews. This formed their richest prize and from the outset they announced their intention to keep the historic city. Standing by the wailing wall General Dayan expressed the united aspiration of his people when he declared, 'we have returned to our holiest of holy places, never to be parted from it again.'[2]

---

1. In 1897, Theodor Herzl, an Austrian journalist, called together the first Zionist Congress in Basle, Switzerland. Part of the resolution passed at that time reads: 'Zionism strives to create for the Jewish people a home in Palestine secured by public law.'

2. 'Jerusalem. Old City – an unexpected by-product of the campaign – has also fired the enthusiasm of all Israelis, whether orthodox or agnostic, in a way that no other event could have. Dayan's statement that it has been recovered "never to be parted with" has hit a chord in every Jewish heart. But, as a Leeds born and bred Israeli told me, "it has existed all the time waiting to be released".' Richard Johns. *Financial Times*. 13 June 1967.

Many Christians have hesitated to assert the fulfilment of the declaration of Jesus: 'Jerusalem shall be trodden down of the Gentiles, until the times of the Gentiles be fulfilled.' Luke 21 : 24. Yet the fact that Gentile domination over Jerusalem has been terminated is inescapable. Adequate time has elapsed to confirm Israel's possession of the Old City. This is reflected in the words of General Chaim Hertzog who said, 'Jerusalem has to be considered separately. No conceivable government that might emerge in Israel would be prepared to cede Israel's position on Jerusalem. The historical associations for the Jewish people of this city through the ages, its significance as the holiest place in Judaism, made it unthinkable for the average Israeli to consider any solution other than the existing one of a united capital city. The Israeli Government has guaranteed complete freedom of worship for all faiths, and protection and virtual autonomy of the Holy Places of all denominations. This presents the most enlightened and liberal policy in the Holy City for the past 2,000 years, since the Romans captured it from the Jews.'[1] The opportunity has not been wasted. The Israelis have united new Jerusalem with the old. The war of words continues especially in the newspapers. Whole-page adverts have appeared in *The Times* calling for another Balfour – a Balfour for displaced Arabs! One correspondent has summed up the position in realistic terms saying, 'There is something slightly ridiculous about the heated exchanges which take place almost daily in your columns, between Arabist and Zionist. The discrepancy between thought and action, between the soundings-off of the various Ambassadors and the stark reality of the Israeli presence, is quite astonishing. The great debate continues

---

1. General Hertzog over B.B.C. reported in *The Listener*, 28 September 1967.

in the pages of a foreign newspaper, while thousands of miles away the situation remains unchanged, unaffected. History provides an excellent parallel – the seizure of Silesia in 1740 by Frederick the Great of Prussia. It took half a century and three wars before Austria became reconciled to the loss; but Silesia was never returned. Will the Arab states take as long to realize the truth of Montaigne's dictum, that "we must accept that which we cannot alter"? There is genuine tragedy in all the waste, the bloodshed, the misery, which results from the refusal to accept what is, rightly or wrongly, accomplished fact.'[1] After nearly two thousand years of Gentile domination we may now say that Jerusalem belongs to, and is governed by Israel.[2] Is it right to conclude that the 'times of the Gentiles' have now come to an end? That question is important since our Lord drew attention to it. An attempt is made to expound the meaning of 'the times of the Gentiles' in Chapter 11.

The territorial restoration of Israel and the capture of Jerusalem in particular has greatly revived interest in the subject of Israel as a whole. No other nation squeezes so many drastic problems into so confined a space. Apart from having to forge a united nation out of an immigrant population representing more languages and backgrounds than any other country in the world, there is the constant problem of survival. The soldier on the cover of this book carries a lethal weapon, a grim reminder that the happy expression on his face can only be maintained by unrelenting vigil. He is surrounded by at least four Arab states bent on the total annihilation of his country. Israel cannot

---

1. Jonathan J. Goldberg, Trinity Hall, Cambridge in *The Times*, 22 May 1968.
2. In actual fact Jerusalem was not fully under Jewish control at the time of Christ. See chapter on Jerusalem.

afford to be caught off guard. Military expenditure is enormous.[1]

Every able bodied man up to the age of fifty-five serves two to four weeks annually in the active reserves. Unmarried women and childless wives form part of the reserve until the age of thirty-four. All eighteen-year-olds are drafted, the men for two years and unmarried girls for eighteen months. Within forty-eight hours 300,000 men can be mobilized. It is unrealistic to say that this is not necessary as the Israelis declare, 'Our neighbours can lose many times and survive. We are outnumbered forty to one. We cannot afford to lose once. Our survival depends on victory every time – for we have no place to hide.' Will this young nation survive? Many ask this question.

Israel with an approximate Jewish population of 2,400,000 is related to eleven million other Jews dispersed throughout ninety nations. This relationship of homeland with brethren so widely spread is unique. The bonds are strong, especially in time of peril. Imagination has been quickened by the diversity of Jews involved in immigration; black Felasha Jews from Ethiopia, white Jews from England, Cochin Jews from India, light-brown Algerians rubbing shoulders with barrow boys from Bulgaria. Large groups have come from Rumania and Poland while Russian and German Jews have played a leading role. From every corner of the globe they have returned, some in dramatic circumstances such as the massive airlift of 45,000 Jews from the Yemen known as 'Operation Magic

---

1. The Jews of the diaspora contributed the colossal total of 1,500 billion dollars (roughly the total cost) towards the Six-day war, according to an unofficial estimate. *The Daily Telegraph* 13 May 1968. It is believed that 30 per cent of the gross national product was spent on security and defence on Israel for 1969, the highest percentage in the world.

Carpet', in which the immigrants returned with a deep conviction that their forebears should have done so at the time of Nehemiah some 2,400 years ago. Others such as 99,000 survivors and escapees from Nazi concentration camps have bitter memories of the past.

One has only to examine labels of books on Israel in local libraries to find that a large number of titles are popular. Every aspect of natural Israel seems to be covered – geography, politics, sociology, tourism, history, Zionism,[1] the recovery of the Negev, the Hebrew University, the Dead Sea Scrolls, the recent wars, and even a variety of biographical material on General Moshe Dayan.

But relatively little is to be found which grapples with problems related to the spiritual destiny of Israel.

The survival of the Jews is mysterious. The attempt to destroy them many years ago in the time of Esther is mysterious. The mass murder of the Jews, which they refer to as the Holocaust, is mysterious. Even the question 'what is a Jew?' is mysterious. This is reflected in the writings of many Jewish authors. For instance Ben Ami asks, 'Is Judaism a religion? Is it a nation? Is it a national

---

1. Zionism was defined by the 23rd Congress in Jerusalem in 1951 as follows: 'The task of Zionism is the consolidation of the State of Israel, the ingathering of the exiles in Eretz Israel and the fostering of the unity of the Jewish people.'

There is an organization known as the Jewish Agency which is linked up with the World Zionist Organization and which has offices at Rex House, 4–12 Regent Street, London, S.W.1. The Jewish Agency is responsible for the following major tasks in Israel: 1 The organization of Jewish immigration to Israel. 2 The reception of Jewish immigrants in Israel and assistance to them to find their place in the economy. 3 The settlement of new immigrants on the land. 4 The care of youth and children among the immigrants (Youth Aliyah). 5 Land amelioration and afforestation by the Jewish National Fund. This information has been quoted from *The Jewish Year Book 1968*.

religion? Or are the Jews a religious nationality? This philosophic-historic problem has been debated by Jewish and non-Jewish thinkers and scholars everywhere, and the answers have been as diverse as those who pondered the questions. Obviously no answer can be found until there is agreement on the definition of the terms "nation", "people", and "religion". We are giving this problem serious attention in Israel, as are the best Jewish thinkers in the United States and other centers of the Jewish Diaspora. But we have not been, and I doubt if we ever will be, able to define precisely who we are. Perhaps this uncertainty is in itself an indication of our unique status. Perhaps the feeling of being Jewish, together with our awareness of the great history of the Jewish tradition and its spiritual heritage, as well as the common memory of persecution and, at present, the concrete link with the Jewish State of Israel – perhaps all of these, together, serve to unite the Jews of the world.'[1] The greatest mystery of all is that to which Paul refers in the eleventh chapter of Romans when he declares to the Gentiles that he would not have them ignorant of this mystery, "that blindness in part is happened to Israel until the fulness of the Gentiles be come in." In other words the real mystery of Israel concerns God's plan for them in the future. This volume is almost wholly devoted to getting to grips with this, the greatest mystery, the spiritual restoration of Israel.

To do this it has been essential to establish a sound basis upon which to work; essential too, to establish beyond all

---

1. Ben Ami in *Between Hammer and Sickle*, p. 48. This problem was highlighted by the case of a monk by the name of Brother Daniel who demanded the right of entry into Israel claiming that though converted to Christianity he was a Jew under the rabbinical definition, that is a person born of a Jewish mother. The Court rejected his claim. Anyone can acquire Israel citizenship after three years' residence, whereas all Jews are recognized upon entry to the country.

shadow of doubt that Paul really meant Israel, the Jewish Israel, in Romans eleven. That chapter is by far the most important concerning the future of Israel to be found in the Bible. Those readers who are already persuaded that the principles upon which this work is based are reliable and who are already convinced that Paul really means the Jews in Romans eleven, may well begin reading at chapter nine. The early chapters (unavoidably technical in places) are included for the unconvinced.

Once it is confirmed from the text that Israel will experience a spiritual revival in the future further questions arise. How will this come to pass? What will it mean to the world? When will it happen? These questions are answered from the Bible before examination is made of Israel today.

Is the time at hand? Is Israel shortly to be restored? Will they recognize their Redeemer? Was the attempt to destroy the Jews devil-inspired in view of their impending restoration? Have the times of the Gentiles been fulfilled? About details we may not be so sure but much which is basic to Paul's teaching can be established with certainty. If the material which follows quickens interest in Bible-study and creates interest in the spiritual salvation of the Jewish people, then it will have served its main purpose.

Oswald T. Allis has expressed the dangers inherent in expounding the prophetic scriptures as follows: 'The great temptation to which the interpreter of the Word is constantly exposed is to invest his own interpretations of Scripture with the authority of Scripture itself, and to assert that those who do not accept his interpretation of God's Word reject God's holy Word itself. This temptation is especially great in dealing with the subject of prophecy. The dogmatism with which many writers on unfulfilled prophecy express themselves regarding things to come is deplorable. The facility with which they ignore the views of all who differ from them is inexcusable. And the finality with which they put forth their prophetic programmes has a tendency to discredit the whole subject of prophecy in the eyes of thoughtful and judicious students of the Bible.'[1]

We need therefore to proceed with caution. It is not possible here to outline the principles of prophecy in detail. Patrick Fairbairn (1805–1874) has done that in his classic *The Interpretation of Prophecy*,[2] a work which breathes the spirit of excellence and which might well be regarded as essential reading on this subject. Here we can briefly refer to major points of consideration only and at the outset need to inquire into the nature of prophecy.

---

1. *Prophecy and the Church*, Pres. and Ref. Pub. Co. 1945. p. 53. See Appendix B – 'The Misuse of Prophecy', for examples.
2. 532 pp. Banner of Truth, £1.25

What is prophecy?

The word *prophet* from the Hebrew word *nabi* means one who breathes out or who reveals the mind, will or message of God. The prophet was God's mouthpiece. He spoke from God to the people in contrast to the priest who spoke for, or who pleaded the cause of the people before God. The prophet was the instrument by which the nature and attributes of God were revealed. He was particularly concerned with establishing and confirming the bond between God and his people. The prophet was also sometimes concerned with foretelling the future purpose of God.

Prophecy then is nothing more or less than the revelation of the mind and purpose of God through his servants the prophets. The two great prophets are Moses[1] and the Lord Jesus Christ. Supremely they have revealed the will and plan of God to mankind. The Scriptures of the Old and New Testaments contain all that God deems necessary for believers. The purpose of these prophecies was to provide us with all the materials of light, comfort, inspiration, direction and encouragement that we need.

Known to God are all his works from the foundation of the world. Had he thought it wise, he could have revealed everything to the early saints such as Abel, Noah or Isaac. But he told them very little about the future. Prediction formed only a small fraction of what God revealed to the early saints. In the first five books of the Bible (which despite the contradictions of critics we attribute to Moses)

---

1. Moses was unique among the Old Testament prophets for the following reasons. 1. He did not have to receive revelation by dreams and visions. 2. He could speak to God directly as man speaks to man. 3. He was not physically prostrated by this contact as were the others like Ezekiel, Isaiah and Daniel. 4. Moses had continual access to God in this way. Num. 12: 6–8. Deut. 18: 15.

God revealed what he planned to accomplish in redemption; but only in broadest outline.

The conflict between the believing church and Satan's hosts, which forms the detailed theme of the book of Revelation, is announced with few words in the first messianic promise of the Bible. Gen. 3: 15. It is declared that the power of Satan is to be crushed by one who will be born of the woman. Little detail is provided.

Likewise prediction of the future events is very limited in the case of Abraham. He receives intimation that his progeny will be innumerable and that through his seed all nations of the earth will be blessed. Jacob predicts the coming of the Messiah who will spring from Judah. Gen. 49: 10. Few details are given.

Moses, apart from the definite statement that in due time Jehovah will raise up another prophet like to himself, says little which is precise concerning the future. Deut. 18: 15. In fact the false prophet Balaam is given as much when it comes to recorded prediction of a precise nature. Num. 24: 16–19.

From all this we learn that God's purpose in providing only a few glimpses into the future is ethical or moral. Prophecy does not consist of predictions merely for us to know the future beforehand. 'Prophecy is not proleptic history' says Charles Hodge, 'it is not designed to give us the knowledge of the future which history gives us of the past. Great events are foretold; but the mode of their occurrence, their details, and their consequences, can only be learned by the event.'[1] We see then that as time goes on more and more spiritual truth concerning the future is revealed, until in the later prophets, such as Isaiah and Malachi, we find whole chapters devoted to detailed descriptions of the Messiah. These are given with spiritual

---

1. *Commentary on Romans*, p. 374.

ends in view. With few exceptions political details are not predicted. Enough is provided all the way through to sustain, edify and comfort the people of God; but no more. Dabbling with future events merely for the sake of satisfying speculative interest is never encouraged. Slowly but surely God's purpose to redeem on an ever increasing scale is unveiled until God's purpose to redeem multitudes from all nations, tribes and kindreds is fully revealed in the New Testament. Note that salvation on a world-wide scale was implied to Abraham, Gen. 12: 3, made known to Moses, Deut. 32: 21, and plainly stated to Isaiah, Is. 49: 6.

Prophecy is ethical in its purpose

Having shown that the predictive element forms only a small part of prophecy – God's Word to men through men – it is important to stress that always we need to look for a moral purpose when God reveals some aspect of the future. Why does he reveal things to come? Invariably the reason is that we might be comforted in the certain triumph of the Gospel, or because we need to be stirred to action and strive for the fulfilment of the promises.

B. B. Warfield declares that 'all prophecy is ethical in its purpose and that ethical ends control not only what shall be revealed in general, but also the details of it and. the very form which it takes'.[1] He is saying that God takes into account the effect that a knowledge of the future will have on his people, and that he is therefore careful in the minutest detail about the way he reveals future events. Patrick Fairbairn points out that our Lord did not even hint at the restoration of the Jews.[2] Apart

---

1. *Bibl. and Theol. Studies.* p. 470.
2. *Inter. of Prop.* p. 249.

from being wrong in his facts at this point, which is very unusual for Fairbairn (Luke 13: 35 and 21: 24 show that our Lord did hint at the restoration of his own people) it must be remembered that it would hardly be in keeping with the tenor of what was happening, for our Lord to minister comforting promises of future restoration to that generation of Jews who were in the act of rejecting him. No; that revelation is left to Paul, who composes the whole prediction of the eleventh of Romans in such a way, that only those who are concerned enough really to ponder and study it, will apprehend its full significance.

These promises proclaiming certainty that the Gospel is destined to triumph in the earth are not given to make Christians lazy or fatalistic. Their purpose is to quicken initiative, renew hope, stir vision and promote action. It is possible to prove that the great missionary awakening of the nineteenth century was rooted and grounded in Puritan theology which was essentially post-millennial. Most of the pioneer missionaries were gripped and inspired by God's promises to fill the earth with a knowledge of his glory. Hence we see illustrated the true moral and ethical purpose of prophecy – an emphasis which urgently needs to be restored to the Church today.

Prophetic teachings which imply that no substantial world-wide victories can be won for the Gospel until Jesus reigns physically from Jerusalem have been harmful in the extreme. The moral effect of such teaching is stultifying and negative. Worse still is the teaching that nothing awaits us now but indescribable tribulation. The ethical effect of such statements is to paralyse, rather than quicken, long-term missionary endeavour. Verses such as 'lo I am with you *always*, even unto the end of the world', and 'he must reign, till he hath put all enemies under his feet', and such prayers as, 'thy kingdom come, thy will be done on earth as it is in heaven' indicate that we should be optimistic concerning the triumph of the Gospel. Such prophecies as, 'I will give thee for a light to the Gentiles that thou mayst be my salvation unto the end of the earth', Is. 49: 6, should fill us with unquenchable zeal to spread the Gospel near and far; to every creature of all tribes and kindreds of the world.

The Jews themselves believe that according to the Old Testament the temple will again be erected and its worship re-established. Throughout the centuries there have been orthodox Jews who have besought God three times a day to 'renew our days as they once were', – a plea for the restoration of the temple. S. M. Lehrman, a former London rabbi, now living in Jerusalem, has written in the *Jewish Chronicle* urging the building of a new temple on the traditional site. His plea is not 'for the restoration of sacrifices and a priestly order', but for a temple 'in which all could worship irrespective of creed'. There are some evangelicals[1] who go much further than the Jews in their expectation of Jewish restoration. According to them a passage like that of Ezekiel, chapters 40–48, must be taken literally.[2] The temple will, therefore, (according to them) be rebuilt in proportions so large that an earthquake is expected to prepare the site for it. The priesthood and the sacrifices will be reinstituted and the Jews will become the most privileged nation in the world. From his throne in Jerusalem Christ will reign over the earth.

Because views such as these prevail it is necessary to define some basic principles in respect of prophecy as it relates to the Jews in particular.

---

1. See section titled 'Dispensationalism' in Appendix A – Different Prophetic Views.
2. Patrick Fairbairn shows that this passage must *not* be taken literally. *Commentary on Ezekiel*, pp. 431–502.

1. The priesthood, sacrifices and rituals of the Old Testament have found their fulfilment in the Messiah and therefore no restoration of Judaistic practices can please God.

The epistle to the Hebrews clearly teaches that Christ, superior both to Moses and Aaron, has fulfilled all the institutions which came through them. It is wrong therefore to look for the restoration of any Judaistic priesthood, sacrifices or rituals. For by one offering he (Jesus) has perfected for ever them that are sanctified. Heb. 10: 14. Any further sacrifice whether a Romish mass or a Jewish sacrifice, is an insult to the perfection of Christ's atonement and therefore an abomination to God.

Moreover Christ has fulfilled the types of the Old Testament – the Tabernacle and Temple. We cannot therefore expect God to accept, or in any way be pleased with, the re-erection of any thing which has been abrogated.

In addition to Hebrews there is the testimony of the epistle to the Galatians which is, in itself, a monument erected to end any idea of Judaistic additions to the gospel of justification by faith only.

2. 'The wall of partition' between Jews and Gentiles has been broken down for ever.

In Christ there is absolute equality. No provision is made for converted Jews to occupy a place of special privilege. That Jews and Gentiles are on the same equal footing is clear: as Paul says, 'There is neither Jew nor Greek, there is neither bond nor free, there is neither male nor female: for ye are all one in Christ Jesus.' Gal.3: 28. And referring to the demolition of the barrier between Jews and Gentiles: he declares, 'That at that time ye (Gentiles) were without Christ being aliens from the commonwealth of Israel, and strangers from the covenants of promise, having no hope, and without God in the world: But now in Christ Jesus ye who sometimes were far off are made nigh by the blood of Christ. For he is our peace, who hath made both one, and hath broken down the middle wall of partition between us.' Eph. 2: 12–14.

There is therefore no place for pride among converted Jews. The apostles, themselves converted Jews, renounced any special status on account of their lineal descent from Abraham.

In the event of the conversion of the Jews, the only distinction open to them will be that available to all Christians, namely, the honour of faithful service. Paul said that he laboured more abundantly than the other apostles because of the grace of God in him. Although it was an advantage to him to be a Jew he never asserted any superiority of status over Gentile believers on that account.

3. There is only one Church from the beginning to the end of time.

The Gospel Church is not a different Church from that which existed in the Old Testament period. The same Church of God which was confined almost exclusively to Jews now includes believers from all nations.

Believing Gentiles have been brought in and joined to believing Israel. The Gentiles, who were 'afar off', are said to be 'made nigh by the blood of Christ'. They are 'no more strangers and foreigners, but fellow-citizens with the saints (the believing Jews) and of the household of God'. Eph. 2: 13, 19.

Our Lord spoke of one fold and one shepherd, and of other sheep which he had to gather and bring. John 10: 16. Again, it was predicted that Jesus should die not only for the Jewish nation, but that 'he should gather together in one the children of God that were scattered abroad'. John 11: 52.

One Church is described in Ephesians. 'There is one body, and one Spirit, . . . one Lord, one faith and one baptism.' Eph. 4: 4, 5. No provision is made for a separate Jewish church. 'Abraham is the father of all who believe,' Jews and Gentiles alike. Rom. 4: 11.

4. The style of language used in prophecy must be carefully examined.

Great care must be taken in the interpretation of any passage to determine whether the prophet is speaking in literal or symbolic terms. What meaning did the words have to those to whom it was directed at the time of its utterance? If directed to Jews – and we should bear in mind that almost all our Lord's words were directed to Jews – how would they understand the phraseology? What was the purpose or reason for the prophecy? All these factors must be taken into account.

We will take an example from the New Testament which is often discussed: 'When the Son of man cometh will he find faith on the earth?' Luke 18: 8. Let us apply the principle stated in the heading to this text.

Is the language literal or symbolic? *Answer*: The language is literal although it must not be assumed that the word 'cometh' applies only to the second coming at the end of the world, as we shall see.[1]

What meaning did the words have to those to whom it

---

1. The Puritans did not confine the meaning of Christ's coming to his second coming only. For instance John Owen in expounding upon the Son of Man 'coming in a cloud, with power and great glory' shows that this refers to the destruction of Jerusalem. Vol. II., p. 139, Goold ed. So also Marcellus Kik in Matt. 24. This is a factor of the greatest importance since it is possible to misinterpret the Olivet discourse in such a way that the whole thing becomes confused. Our Lord is asked two questions which he answers in order: first the one, then the other. We must not ascribe what belongs to the second coming to Jerusalem, simply because to our Western minds the language seems to fit the second coming so well.

was directed? *Answer*: Our Lord had just been warning them by referring to different *days* of his personal coming in judgment: the days of Noah, and Lot. He might come swiftly at any time in judgment – as indeed he did to Jerusalem in A.D. 70. But especially will he come at the end of the world. Jesus then continues to encourage his disciples to pray and uses the parable of the widow and the unjust judge to describe the kind of faith that he requires. She did not despair. She kept persevering until her petition was answered. Now whenever Jesus comes, whether in judgment on a nation, or at the end of the world, will he find faith of this character? Will he find faith like that of the widow who persevered? That this question would be understood in a local sense is undisputable since 'on the earth' to the Jews would mean nothing more or less than their own land. For instance when Isaiah uses the phrase 'the whole earth', Is. 28: 22, he refers only to the inhabitants of Canaan. Instances can be quoted from the Talmud to prove that this claim is correct.

What was the purpose or reason for this statement? *Answer:* Our Lord did not ask this question with the intention that we should answer it in reference to the end of the world: yes, you will find persevering faith: no, you will not find persevering faith. That he will find true faith is clear because he has just been saying that one will be left and another taken. But the kind of faith that he will find is unknown to us. We cannot answer his question. Why then did he ask it? We come back to what was explained in the previous chapter. God always has a moral end in view. This question, 'will he find faith' is calculated to stir up self-examination. If he suddenly comes to call me into his presence will I have faith; true persevering faith? That is a question you and I must answer without delay.

The prophecies of the Old Testament were addressed to Jews. Many passages in the Gospels, particularly the

Olivet discourse, Luke, ch. 21, Matt. ch. 24, Mark, ch. 13, and the passage commented on above were directed specifically to Jews. How did they understand the style of language used? Many have made arbitrary interpretations without investigating what the words meant to the Jews at the time of utterance. This has been a main cause of error in the area of prophecy.

This subject is a large one. Much could be said on the difference of styles used. Are the words prose, poetry or apocalyptic? There are also grammatical, historical and contextual considerations. Here elementary matters only have been considered, one more of which needs to be mentioned.

5. The pre-eminence and finality of the New Testament revelation must be maintained.

Augustine stated this matter aptly when he declared, 'In the Old Testament the New is concealed; in the New Testament the Old is revealed.'

It is obvious that we should always proceed directly to the clearest passages first and in the light obtained from them seek to interpret the difficult passages. By the New Testament we interpret and understand the Old. Even in the New Testament we do wisely to establish truth from the clear literal statements of the epistles before attempting to interpret the book of Revelation. Calvin is reputed to have said that he did not understand Revelation, yet some with only a fraction of his ability have based their whole system on the highly figurative twentieth chapter of Revelation.

In a study of the future of Israel we can do no better than to examine that extended New Testament passage which deals in literal and specific terms concerning their future, namely the eleventh chapter of Romans, to which we now proceed.

29

THE THREE GATHERINGS

4

Paul's epistle to the Romans is the greatest of all his letters; it forms the most systematic and definitive document describing true Christianity that we possess. Paul wrote this letter from Corinth in the year A.D. 58, just before his visit to Jerusalem. He much desired to reach Rome but was unable to do so being dogged by adverse circumstances. This turned out to be of immense benefit to posterity, for, deprived of the opportunity to expound Christian truth to the Romans in person, Paul resolved to do so by way of a letter. The Roman epistle is the outcome. With the exception of Ephesians, Paul's epistles deal mainly with problems which perplexed the Christians to whom they were addressed. The uniqueness of Romans is seen in the uninterrupted line of thought setting out the doctrine of Justification by Faith. This is the theme right through to the end of the eleventh chapter. Thereafter, in the closing chapters, Paul applies the doctrine to the various spheres in which the Christian finds himself. We might view the epistle as follows:

Romans:	**Justification**
Chapters 1–11.	
Chapter 1.	Introduction vv. 1–15. Justification introduced vv. 16–18. The Gentiles under sin vv. 19–32.
Chapter 2.	The Jews also under sin.
Chapter 3.	All are under sin vv. 1–20. God's provision of justification explained vv. 21–31.
Chapter 4.	Justification in the Old Testament.

Chapter 5.	The fruits of justification vv. 1–11. Justification as it applies to the redeemed race vv. 12–21.
Chapter 6.	Objections against justification answered.
Chapter 7.	Justification and the moral law.
Chapter 8.	Justification and life in the Holy Spirit. Justification and God's plan vv. 28–39.
Chapters 9–11.	Justification viewed against the background of human history from the beginning to the end of time.

From the ninth to the eleventh chapters the most complete treatment concerning salvation as it applies to Jews and Gentiles as distinct groups is set before us.

Paul begins by sorrowing over the fact of Jewish failure but goes on to prove that this was in God's purpose. The apostle upholds the truth of Divine Sovereignty in the ninth chapter but lays equal stress upon the fact of Human Responsibility in the tenth.

In the eleventh chapter he spurns the suggestion that the rejection of the Jews is final. The time will come when 'all Israel' will be saved. The faith and obedience of the Gentiles are to be the means of restoration of the Jews. Verses 11–32. It is clear from the eleventh chapter that there are three distinct periods of salvation. We will refer to them as *The Three Gatherings*.

The First Gathering – Jews

Throughout the period, from Abraham to Christ, salvation was confined mainly to the Jews. Wherever they went they built synagogues and proselytized among the Gentiles. The effect of this activity is clearly reflected in the number of proselytes from innumerable nations gathered in Jerusalem at the time of Pentecost. But if we

31

go back hundreds of years from the time of Pentecost to the time of entry into Canaan we find Rahab the harlot of Jericho, and her family being brought into the number of the redeemed. And the salvation of Nineveh from threatened destruction might be regarded as typical of times to come in respect of salvation on a large scale among the Gentiles.[1] In general, however, it must be admitted that the period of the first ingathering was mainly confined to the salvation of Jews.

The turning point arrived when Jesus 'came unto his own, and they received him not'. Those Jews who did believe were numerous enough to constitute a band of disciples which turned the world upside down. From them we have received the New Testament. But as the years passed it became clear that the great majority of Jews had rejected their Messiah. Fewer and fewer Jews believed. In the meantime the Gospel was carried to the Gentile nations to become their possession for the centuries that followed.

The Second Gathering – Gentiles

Despite persecution the advance of the Christian Faith during the early centuries was irresistible. Eventually under Constantine it became the established religion. The seeds of apostasy had already been sown however, and there ensued a falling away so great, that darkness prevailed for many centuries. Nevertheless a faithful persecuted minority of true believers always remained. Heroic

---

1. Not many commentators on Jonah provide analysis of whether the repentance of Nineveh was just a general kind of turning away from gross evil or whether it was repentance to salvation. I am of the opinion that it was repentance to salvation for a large number. My reasons for this are: 1. God has gracious purposes of salvation in view in sending special preachers to call men to repentance. 2. We have no reason to suppose that there were no agencies diffusing the knowledge of salvation in Nineveh.

attempts were made to reform the Church and men like John Hus of Bohemia, and Savonarola of Florence, were burned at the stake for preaching the truth.

It was not until the Reformation led by men such as Tyndale, Luther, Zwingli and Calvin that a new period of Gospel prosperity was ushered in. For many years expansion was confined mainly to Europe and North America. During the nineteenth century however, missionary effort took on new dimensions until at the present time there exists a network of missions and churches throughout the free world, together with an underground church of unknown proportions in those countries under the shadow of the red flag such as Russia, China and the nations of Eastern Europe.

Apart from the apostolic period it is to be noted that the overwhelming majority of converts have been Gentiles. The main leaders, writers, reformers and missionaries have been Gentiles.

The period from the times of the apostles until today has been an ingathering of souls which has gradually increased in volume – an ingathering confined almost exclusively to Gentiles.

The Third Gathering

Through Hebrew Christian instrumentality we Gentiles received the Gospel at the beginning. Through Gentile instrumentality the Jews will embrace the Gospel once more. 'Through your mercy they may obtain mercy.' Rom. 11: 31. This will, according to Romans eleven, result in the third gathering; a gathering of Jews and Gentiles together. This final gathering may well be an ingathering of much greater proportions than the second, which in turn has been much greater than the first.

'The web of Providence' says Charles Hodge, in his

commentary on Romans, 'is wonderfully woven, good and evil is made with equal certainty to result in the promotion of God's gracious and glorious designs.'

The evil of sin is exposed and seen in the decay of the Gentile world. Babylonian glory, Greek wisdom and Roman power could not attain to salvation. Sin reigned to death over the Gentiles until Christ came. Salvation was confined mainly to the Jews. Their privileges, however, made them proud; this led to their rejection of the Messiah. Consequently they have, through the centuries, been left to their own devices. The Gentiles who before wallowed in corruption and superstition have been raised up by grace to receive salvation through the Lamb. The impotence and sin of Jews and Gentiles alike has been proved. Also demonstrated is the fact that salvation is by free grace of God alone.

May the day come quickly when Israel and all the nations cease going about to establish their own righteousness and submit themselves to the grace of God as revealed in the Bible. Then we may witness the third gathering in which large numbers of both Jews and Gentiles will be saved together.

WHAT DOES PAUL MEAN BY 'ALL ISRAEL'?

5

And so all Israel *shall be saved.* Romans 11 : 26.

Having viewed the eleventh chapter of Romans against the general structure of that epistle, and having seen that three periods of ingathering are implied in that chapter, we now come face to face with a factor which is vital to the entire subject. It can be stated as follows.

Romans chapter 11 is regarded as the shining planet of the Bible as far as the future of the Jews is concerned. No other passage can compare with it. Charles Hodge calls it the 'omnium instar' which can be translated, 'the most valuable of all things' or 'worth all the rest'. Yet there are many who claim that Paul is not here speaking of the Jews when he says 'all Israel shall be saved'. Everything hangs on those two words *all Israel.* If the eleventh chapter is the shining planet, then these two words form the most disputed territory of that planet. It is worth our while to investigate this matter carefully.

Several writers have strongly denied that 'all Israel', Rom. 11 : 26, means ethnic[1] Israel – the physical descendants of Abraham or the race of Jews as we know them today. Dr. R. C. H. Lenski, the learned Lutheran New Testament commentator, in his commentary on Romans attempts to prove at all costs, that 'all Israel' does not mean the race of Israel. In doing so he provides little positive exposition of the passage. His commentary stands in strong contrast to that of Professor John Murray. Whereas the latter opens up the text to the full, explaining every

---

1. In using the word *ethnic* the race of Jews by blood descent is meant. The word *ethnic* is not ideal because of its etymology but it is preferable to the word *racial.*

phrase and verse in relationship to the whole, Dr. Lenski's commentary is full of negative arguments. Dr. Lenski maintains that 'all Israel' means all the elect; the spiritual Israel of saved Jews and Gentiles together. He betrays the weakness of his case by inadequate explanation of what Paul means when he uses phrases such as 'they are beloved for the fathers' sakes'. Who are *beloved for the fathers' sakes*? Throughout the chapter Paul is speaking about the people Israel – the race of Jews.

It is inconceivable that Paul should argue that all the elect will be saved. Who would dispute so fundamental a matter? He does labour to prove that the body of Jewish people, 'all Israel', will be saved. There were, and are, many who doubt that!

This particular point is crucial. It is therefore necessary to examine the expression 'all Israel' in detail, before going on to consider the meaning of the other phrases in this passage used by Paul to describe the Israelites as a racial entity.

New Testament usage of the word 'Israel'

It appears that the word 'Israel' is used fifty-one times in the New Testament. In all but three places in which the land of Israel is referred to, the reference is to Israel as a distinct race. Gal. 6: 16, is one exception where the phrase 'the Israel of God' is used to denote all the elect. Typical use of the word 'Israel' is instanced in the case of Simeon, a just and devout Jew of Jerusalem who awaiting 'the consolation *of Israel*', took up the child Jesus into his arms and described him as, 'A light to lighten the Gentiles, and the glory of *thy people Israel*.' 'I have not found so great faith, no not in *Israel*' (not among the Jews), a comment made by our Lord, is another example of the use of the word *Israel*.

This clear distinction between Israel and the Gentiles is maintained throughout the New Testament. The early believers, both converted Jews and Gentiles, were strongly aware of this racial difference. When they read Rom. 11 they would understand 'all Israel' in the context to mean none other than the race of Israelites, the seed of Abraham.

Strong appeal is made by those who interpret 'all Israel' in the spiritual sense as all the elect, to the fact that in Rom. 2: 28, 29, Paul explains that they are not all Jews who are so by physical descent. To be a true Jew there must be circumcision of the heart. Again in chapter 9 Paul declares, 'For they are not all Israel, which are of Israel. . . . the children of the promise are counted for the seed.' Verses 6–8. This important and fundamental truth expressed by the apostle does not alter the fact, even in the slightest degree, that in other passages in the same epistle Paul refers explicitly to the Israelitish race 'my kinsmen according to the flesh: *who are Israelites.*' Rom. 9: 3, 4. When he does refer to physical Israel, numbering himself as one of them – 'I too am an Israelite, of the seed of Abraham, of the tribe of Benjamin' Rom. 11: 1, we cannot doubt that he is speaking in literal, and not spiritual terms, concerning the race of which he physically is a member. Moreover, it is significant that he deals distinctly with Jews and Gentiles as separate racial groups throughout the epistle.

Reference to Romans 11: 24–26

Archibald Hughes is a typical representative of the school who assert that 'all Israel' in Rom. 11: 26 means not ethnic Israel, but all the redeemed; Jews and Gentiles together. His argument is succinctly stated.

Hughes maintains that the adverb 'so', in 'and *so* all Israel shall be saved' refers to the manner, and not the time of Israel's salvation.[1] The 'so', he declares, refers to the way in which 'all Israel' are grafted into the good olive tree. He believes verse 26 refers back to verse 23 and verse 24, omitting verse 25. The sense is then as follows:

verse 23. The Jews, if they do not persist in unbelief will be grafted in, for God is able to graft them in again,

  24. – how much easier it will be to graft the natural branches into their own olive tree,

  26. and *so* all Israel (Gentiles and Jews) shall be saved.

Such a rendering neglects the intervening verse 25 to which verse 26 is linked.[2] The 'and so' with which verse 26 begins indicates a proposition which flows directly from verse 25. It means 'and accordingly'. And 'so' draws out the implication of what immediately precedes it, i.e. *when* (a reference to time) the fulness of the Gentiles has come in, then all Israel shall be saved. It is impossible to divorce the conclusion drawn at the beginning of verse 26 from verse 25. Hughes, therefore, is mistaken in seeking to by-pass verse 25, and wrong in trying to change the 'and so' to refer exclusively to the manner in which Israel is ingrafted into the olive tree instead of allowing it to have its primary meaning – its full dynamic force as a reference to the time when all Israel shall be saved. We can paraphrase as follows:

verse 25. Lest you should be proud, I do not want you Gentile brethren to miss this truth: a hardening which is temporary has befallen Israel which shall last until the fulness of the Gentiles be gathered in

---

1. *A new heaven and a new earth*, page 50.
2. 'Since verse 26 is a parallel or correlative statement the denotation of "Israel" must be the same as in verse 25. It is of ethnic Israel Paul is speaking in verse 25 and Israel in that place cannot possibly include the Gentiles.' Professor John Murray. *Romans*, volume 2, page 96. 'It is impossible to entertain an exegesis which takes "Israel" here in verse 26 in a different sense from "Israel" in verse 25.' Dr. F. F. Bruce.

26. and so accordingly when this comes to pass all Israel will be saved, for it is written, the Deliverer will come out of Zion and he will remove ungodliness from Jacob.

The reasoning is clear. When the fulness of the Gentiles is come in, blinded Israel shall have her ungodliness removed to become saved Israel. All Israel cannot mean the total number of saved Gentiles and saved Jews. Such an interpretation is strained and unnatural in face of the governing interest of the apostle in this passage.

The word 'all' in 'all Israel' should not stumble us. Throughout the Bible the word 'all' is used in a general sense and does not necessarily mean every single person. For instance, in Matt. 4: 24 we read 'that they brought unto him *all* sick people'. This does not mean every sick person without exception. It means a great many, or the majority of sick people in that part where Jesus was ministering.

So in Rom. 11: 26 'all Israel' does not mean that every single Jew in the world will be converted or that every Jew in the land of Israel will experience personal salvation. It *does* mean that a sufficient number of Jews will embrace the Messiah so that the world will acknowledge that *they as a people* have become Christian.

The general use of the word 'all' in verse 32 should be noted: 'For God hath concluded them all in unbelief, that he might have mercy upon all.' We could not say here that God has concluded every single Jew in unbelief as that would deny verse 25, where we are told 'blindness in part' is happened to Israel. A few Jews have believed. So when Paul says that God will have mercy upon all the Jews he means it in a general sense as referring to the Jewish people generally.

It should be apparent both from the passage as a whole, and from the immediate context, that it is impossible to expound 'Israel' in verse 26 in any other way than *ethnic* Israel. Moreover, phrases are used throughout the passage to describe Israel which confirm the fact that ethnic Israel is meant in verse 26. We shall now examine some of these.

note:
  William Hendriksen in his book *Israel and the Bible* (see bibliography) lists Calvin, van Leeuwen and Jacobs as those who agree with Lenski's interpretation, which we have examined, i.e. 'all Israel' refers to the total number of elect Jews and Gentiles. This position we are in the process of rejecting on the grounds that it does violence to the context. Expositors who take 'all Israel' to mean ethnic Israel are Doekes, Denny, Erdman, Gifford, Greijdanus, Sanday and Headlam, van Andel, Voigt and Vos. To these should be added those listed on page 150ff. There is another view not discussed in these pages to which Hendriksen himself subscribes and which he elaborates in *Israel and the Bible*. 'All Israel' he takes as the accumulative number of elect Jews in history. Not a few Dutch companions (and others) join him in this position, namely, Barthing, Bavinck, Berkhof, Hallesby, Odland, Ridderbos and Volbeda. Hendriksen maintains that the whole context concerns the believing Jewish remnant. But surely this is impossible since from 11:12 onwards Paul is reasoning by way of contrast, the terms of which are plainly stated in verses 12 and 15. The conclusion is reached at verse 32 whereupon the apostle bursts out in praise.
  But Hendriksen ignores verses 12 and 15 as he does 27 and 29. The accumulation theory is better than trying to fit Gentiles into the 'all Israel' of verse 26. Nevertheless it too falls flat, since it ignores the upward sweep towards a climax in Paul's reasoning. With rising crescendo the apostle brings to light the plan of God. Such is God's wisdom revealed in using the interaction of Jews and Gentiles upon each other, and such is the plenitude and magnitude of it all, that an overwhelming acclamation of joy and praise is called for. To this Paul gives expression in the concluding verses. Our interpretation is consistent with this joyful conclusion whereas the others are not.

'And so all Israel shall be saved.' This sentence, character-ized by finality, forms the conclusion of an argument which Paul begins in the tenth chapter at verse 19. 'Did not Israel know?' Israel did know. But Israel rejected the overtures of the Gospel. Rom. 10: 21. Therefore has God cast away his people? God forbid! Paul firmly rejects the suggestion. He then begins to argue the case for Israel's restoration which leads up to the statement of verse 26, 'And so all Israel shall be saved.' The apostle does not conclude there however. He goes on to provide further reasons as to why Israel should be saved. Throughout he is pleading the restoration of *ethnic* Israel. This is the object in view and from this he does not digress.

An examination of the phrases used at different points within this section of Paul's letter will: 1. Confirm that the whole passage leads up to the conclusion that all Israel will be saved. 2. Underline the certainty of Israel's spiritual recovery, and 3. Cast light upon the people of Israel as they are viewed by God.

1. A disobedient and gainsaying people. Rom. 10: 21

In order to support their view those who reject the spiritual restoration of Israel, quote texts such as, 'the king-dom shall be taken away from you and shall be given to a nation bringing forth the fruits thereof' Matt. 21: 43, and the curse of Jesus upon the fig tree. In reference to the fig tree it is noteworthy that Judaism is represented and not the Jewish people as such. Judaism is obsolete. As far as spiritual fruit is concerned Judaism is stone-dead: as dead as the stones in the wailing wall. Self-justifying Judaism stands blasted from the roots to this day. Not one soul has ever been saved by it as Paul declares, 'by the works of the law shall no flesh be justified in his sight.' Jews have been saved by believing the Gospel so that it is wrong to identify the fig tree with the Jews as a people. God has not cast away the race of Israelites, for 'the Lord will not cast off his people'.[1]

'But to Israel he saith, all day long have I stretched forth my hands to a disobedient and gainsaying people.' Does the disobedience of the Jews mean that they will be left in spiritual desolation as a people to the end of time? In answer to this question we must remember the words of Jesus: 'Your house is left unto you desolate – *until* you say, blessed is he that cometh in the name of the Lord.' Luke 13: 35. A terminus or end to this desolation is indicated. In Rom. 11 the apostle goes on to deny the suggestion that Israel's disobedience has resulted in a casting-off which is final and irrevocable. He insists that 'God has not cast away his people which he foreknew.' Rom. 11: 2.

2. A people 'foreknown'. Romans 11: 2.

In Scripture the word foreknow often signifies knowledge accompanied by a decree. 'Him being delivered up by the determinate counsel and foreknowledge of God.' Acts 2: 23. God foreknows everything that comes to pass because he has ordained or predestinated everything before the time. He has done this without being the author of evil.[2]

---

1. See Ps. 94: 14. cf. I Sam. 12: 22. Jer. 31: 37.
2. This subject which many find perplexing is expounded in detail in *The Reformed Doctrine of Predestination* by Dr. Loraine Boettner. p. 228.

'Foreknown' in Romans 11: 2 means (as elsewhere in Scripture) a people fore-loved and fore-chosen. The word 'know' is often used in the Bible as knowing someone with intimate love and affection. Adam 'knew' his wife Eve. To the Corinthians Paul said, 'If any man love God, the same is *known* (loved) of Him.' 'You only have I *known* of all the families of the earth' declares God concerning Israel. Amos 3: 2.

This is the meaning in Rom. 8: 29. 'For whom he did *foreknow*, he also did predestinate to be conformed to the image of his Son.' Believers are saved because of the love of God. He set his love upon Jeremiah saying, 'Before I formed thee in the womb I *knew* thee.' Election has its spring in the love of God. Hence believers are described as 'elect; according to the foreknowledge (love) of God the Father,' I Peter 1: 2.

Israel as a people is loved in this sense. The whole generation that came purified out of the wilderness into Canaan, was holiness to the Lord. They were a saved people. Jer. 2: 3. So the day will come again when 'all Israel shall be saved,' verse 26, because Israel as a people is foreknown of the Lord.

3. A people not irretrievably fallen. Romans 11: 11.

Some sinners whom God has chosen to save continue a long time in unbelief before they are converted. For many years there seems to be little hope for them. Eventually, however, grace prevails. Even though unbelief may have prevailed for decades the day of conversion does eventually dawn.

The same principle applies to the Jews as a nation. Even though they have continued in unbelief for centuries they have not fallen beyond remedy. 'I will' says God, 'for their sakes remember the covenant of their ancestors,

... that I might be their God: I am the Lord.' Lev. 26: 45. The addition of the words 'I am the Lord' reminds us that ultimately salvation is not dependent upon man's will. If it were so, none would be saved, for all are by nature 'at enmity with God'. Rom. 8: 7. Man's will is in bondage and is averse to spiritual things. The natural man cannot comprehend spiritual matters. They are foolishness to him. I Cor. 2: 14. Salvation belongs to God. Because he is the Lord Jehovah, gracious, merciful, faithful, omnipotent, he will raise his fallen people again.

4. A people who shall experience 'fulness'. Romans 11: 12.

From verses 11–15 Paul reasons concerning the fulness of Israel.

It would help at this point to read the text in order to follow Paul's reasoning concerning the 'fall' and the 'fulness' of Israel. Amplified it reads:

> *verse 11.* So I ask, have they so stumbled as to fall irretrievably? God forbid: but by their fall salvation has come to the Gentiles, as to provoke Israel to be jealous.
>
> *12.* Now if their fall has enriched the world, and if Israel's failure has meant riches accruing to the Gentiles, think what enrichment would follow their full reinstatement!
>
> *13.* But I speak to you that are Gentiles. Inasmuch as I am an apostle of the Gentiles, I glorify my ministry.
>
> *14.* In the hope of making my fellow Jews jealous, in order to stir them up and bring them to salvation.
>
> *15.* For if the casting away of the Israelites has led to the reconciling of the world, what shall the receiving again of the Israelites mean, but life from the dead to the Gentiles?

Israel stumbled and fell through rejecting their Messiah. Their loss has been staggering: their failure dreadful. But as 'a fall' is ascribed to Israel in this passage so is the term 'fulness'. The latter means plenitude, completeness or full complement. As all Israel has been marked by unbelief and subsequent desolation so here she is contemplated as restored to faith in Christ. 'Fulness' conveys the idea of thoroughness and completeness. 'Hence' argues John Murray in his commentary at this point, 'nothing less than a restoration of Israel as a people to faith, privilege, and blessing can satisfy the terms of this passage.' He goes on to add, 'the *argument* of the apostle is not, however, the restoration of Israel; it is the blessing accruing to the Gentiles from Israel's "fulness". The "fulness" of Israel, with the implications stated above, is presupposed and from it is drawn the conclusion that the fulness of Israel will involve for the Gentiles a much greater enjoyment of gospel blessing than that occasioned by Israel's unbelief. Thus there awaits the Gentiles, in their distinctive identity as such, gospel blessing far surpassing anything experienced during the period of Israel's apostasy, and this unprecedented enrichment will be occasioned by the conversion of Israel on a scale commensurate with that of their earlier disobedience.'[1]

5. A people to be received. Romans 11 : 15.

The meaning of 'to be received' is illustrated by the parable of the Prodigal Son. As the father received his repentant son so are all received who return to God through Jesus Christ. The Jews are no exception – they are to be received at some time in the future.

---

1. *Romans*, Volume 2, p. 79.

A CALLING THAT IS WITHOUT REPENTANCE

A French Jewish sociologist, Georges Friedmann, has written a book in which the title reflects the extreme pessimism of the writer. It is called *The End of the Jewish People?* The author has comforted himself at least with a question mark. He need not be over-anxious. The Jews have miraculously survived centuries of assault and discouragement. Mysterious reasons lie behind their survival. The expressions used by Paul, which are now to be examined, illustrate the impossibility of annihilating the Hebrew people. God has a future purpose for them which guarantees their survival. Besides pointing to God's purpose with the Jews in the future, the following phrases also confirm the contentions of the previous chapter.

'A holy root.' Romans 11: 16.

It will help to see the force of Paul's reasoning at this point by quoting from the Amplified New Testament.

verse 16. Now if the first handful of dough offered as the firstfruits (Abraham and the patriarchs) is consecrated (holy), so is the whole mass (the nation of Israel); and if the root (Abraham) is consecrated (holy), so are the branches.

17. But if some of the branches were broken off, while you, a wild olive shoot, were grafted in among them to share the richness [of the root and sap] of the olive tree.

18. Do not boast over the branches and pride yourself at their expense. If you boast and feel superior, remember that it is not you that supports the root, but the root (that supports) you.

The Israelites were required to make an offering of the first-fruits of the earth, both in its raw state as a sheaf of newly reaped grain, Lev. 23: 10, 11, and in a prepared state when made into cakes of dough, Num. 15: 19–21. By this offering it was shown that the entire harvest of the season was consecrated to God. The whole was regarded as holy to the Lord.

The reasoning of the apostle is that separation to God of the patriarchs, Abraham, Isaac and Jacob, from the rest of mankind, was a real offering of the first-fruits. In Abraham all families of the earth were to be blessed. Abraham was heir of the world. In God's view, the consecrated nature of the root means the consecration of the whole tree. Branches may be broken off and wild branches grafted in, but the root, and the nation arising out of that root, are consecrated in the eyes of God for all time; consecrated, that is in a covenant sense. Just as God left the nation for 400 years in Egypt and later for many years in Babylon, so he has left them now as a distinct nation in a state of judicial blindness. But as will be shown in the next chapter he will respect his covenant.

The exposition of Elnathan Parr, the Puritan commentator on Romans reads as follows:

Objection: *The nation of the Jews is before called rebellious: how then can it now be called holy?*

Answer: There is a double holiness: First, of regeneration. Secondly, of the covenant: in regard to the first they are rebellious: in regard to the second, they are holy.

This explanation is warranted when we consider the reasoning of Paul concerning the children of believers. I Cor. 7: 14. The children of believers are holy in that they are set apart and dedicated to God. 'Now they are *holy,*' declares Paul, even though we have no absolute certainty

47

that they will believe. On these grounds some ministers baptize the infants of believers.[1]

As touching the election they are beloved for the fathers' sakes. 11:28.

The election here spoken of is not the personal choice of individuals, Rom. 11:5, but the election of a nation. The election is of the nation as a whole in that sense in which no other nation was ever chosen. 'Thou art a holy people unto the Lord thy God: the Lord thy God hath chosen thee to be a special people unto himself.' Deut. 7:6. 'For thou hast confirmed to thyself thy people Israel to be a people unto thee for ever.' II Sam. 7:24.

On the basis of this national election the apostle Peter addressed the children of Israel in these terms: 'Ye are the children of the prophets, and of the covenant which God made with our fathers, saying unto Abraham, And in thy seed shall all the kindreds of the earth be blessed. Unto you first God, having raised up his Son Jesus, sent him to bless you, in turning away every one of you from his iniquities.' Acts 3:25, 26.

Robert Haldane in his commentary on Romans points out that 'the elect' referred to by our Lord in the Olivet discourse refers to national Israel. 'Except those days should be shortened, there should no flesh be saved: but for the elect's sake those days shall be shortened.' Matt. 24:22. Here the elect cannot refer to the Christians, who, heeding our Lord's warning, escaped to the mountains. The meaning is rather that if those days of judgment had not been shortened the Jews would have been destroyed

---

1. Paul K. Jewett, an American Baptist, has written a masterly treatise on the subject of baptism especially as it is related to the covenant. He shows that belief in the covenant relationship of infants is important but *does not* provide a warrant to baptize them.

beyond recovery. Such an event was not allowed, for the
Jews were to be preserved in a corporate sense to be called
in a future age. Their destruction was limited as it was
this century when the plot to destroy them completely was
thwarted in the Allied victory over the Nazi régime. As
God said through Isaiah: 'Destroy it not; for a blessing is
in it: so will I do for my servants' sakes, that I may not
destroy them all.' Is. 65:8. The preservation of the
Israelites through the centuries has been astonishing. Is it
because a copious blessing is to come through them?

When we turn our attention to the phrase, 'beloved for
the fathers' sakes', we are not to think of this in a senti-
mental way; that God looks fondly upon the Jews merely
because they are lineally or physically descended from the
patriarchs. The idea is not that of looking with favour
upon the children of some dear old friend of ours who is
deceased, so as to favour and help those children on
account of an affection for our departed friend, worthy
though that might be. It is because of God's covenant
obligations that he says, 'They are beloved for the fathers'
sakes.' 'Beloved,' says John Murray at this point, 'means
that God has not suspended or rescinded his relation to
Israel as his chosen people in terms of the covenants made
with their fathers. Unfaithful as Israel has been, and
broken off for that reason, yet God still sustains his
peculiar relationship to that nation, a relationship that
will be demonstrated and vindicated in spiritual restoration. Verses 12, 15, 26.'

'In other words' (to use the expression of David Brown
in his commentary on *Romans*) 'the natural Israel – *not*,
"the *remnant* of them according to the election of grace,"
but the NATION, sprung from Abraham according to the
flesh – are still an elect people, and as such, "beloved."
The very same love which chose the fathers, and rested on
the fathers as the parent stem of the nation, still rests on

their descendants at large, and will yet rescue them from unbelief, and reinstate them in the family of God.'

A people with 'gifts and calling of God' that 'are without repentance' 11: 29.

The 'calling of God' means that sovereign act of God whereby he 'called' Abraham to be the father of a peculiar people. 'The gifts' referred to, denote the articles of the covenant which God made with Abraham and confirmed to his seed, reference being made to these gifts in Rom. 9: 4, 5. God has not changed his mind about the spiritual application of the covenant to Israel. He cannot change. 'God is not a man, that he should lie; neither the son of man, that he should repent: hath he not said, and shall he not do it? Hath he spoken, and shall he not make it good?' Num. 23: 19. Paul appeals to the faithfulness of God: 'For what if some of them did not believe? shall their unbelief make the faith of God without effect?' Rom. 3: 3. The latter statement confirms the certainty of God's promise which is to make good the covenant with Abraham; a covenant which embraces his seed to the end of time. Gen. 17: 7, 8.

Conclusion

We have now examined a number of phrases used to describe Israel. The three elaborated upon in this section spell out a future for them and are closely related to God's covenant with the Jews. To that very important matter we now proceed.

GOD'S PROMISE TO REMOVE ISRAEL'S SINS 8

'For this is my covenant unto them when I shall take away their sins.' Romans 11 : 27.

The pivotal question here is whether God's covenant applies to the Jews as a race until this present time or not. Was it abrogated when the Jewish nation rejected Christ as their Messiah? This can only be resolved by inquiry into the meaning of the text, which can be broken up in this way:

1. My covenant: what this covenant is.
2. Its implication: I will take away their sins.
3. To whom it is applied: *with them* when I take away *their* sins.

1. My covenant: what this covenant is

The covenant of God is his sovereign determination to have mercy upon sinners. Note the personal pronoun in the text: 'this is *my* covenant'. This covenant is conceived and established by God himself. It finds its fullest and highest expression in the declaration of God: 'I will be your God, and ye shall be my people.' In order to ensure the eternal security of this relationship with his people, God has, by his own great and holy name, declared that he will change his people inwardly, and so redeem them for all eternity: 'I will put my laws into their minds; and write them in their hearts.' Heb. 8: 10. This is the new covenant.

God's covenant is sometimes called the covenant of grace and sometimes termed the covenant of redemption. These names need not confuse us. Put simply it means that Father, Son and Holy Spirit have a bond together that they will redeem sinners; hence, 'covenant of redemption'. The grounds upon which they would accomplish this is grace: hence, 'covenant of grace'.[1]

What of the covenants mentioned in the Old Testament? How are we to understand these? The answer is that they are steps leading up to the full revelation of God's covenant of grace which finally finds its fullest expression in what we call the new covenant.[2] Various aspects of salvation are highlighted through these covenants which are like sub-headings falling under a major heading.[3]

It will be helpful to view these covenants as follows:

1. The Pre-diluvian covenant with Noah. Gen. 6: 18.	God will preserve mankind and the animal world from total destruction.
2. The Post-diluvian covenant with Noah. Gen. 9: 9–17.	God declares he will never again destroy the whole earth with water. This covenant points to universal preservation in order that there might be a world-wide redemption among the nations.
3. The covenant with Abraham. Gen. 12: 1–3, 15: 5–18, 17: 1–16.	This covenant includes personal promises to Abraham. God will create a new race out of Abraham. All nations will be blessed through Abraham and his seed (from whom the Messiah came). He will give the land of Canaan to this new nation for ever. God's covenant with Abraham

---

1. Grace is commonly known to mean 'unmerited favour'. This idea is inadequate. The grace of God means that he comes in mercy to those who may have positively hated him, rejected him, and been his enemies. There is positive *demerit* in those to whom God comes in sovereign saving mercy. He changes their natures and works a miracle of conversion within them when they really deserve to perish everlastingly.
2. See Heb. 8: 10. cf. Jer. 31: 31–34.
3. For a discussion of the covenant see Berkhof's *Systematic Theology* p. 262–301. There is an extended article by Professor John Murray on the covenant, in *The New Bible Dictionary* (I.V.F.). This is the clearest exposition in brief compass that I have found.

involves the requirement of holiness. The carnal life of the flesh is to be put off: this is illustrated in circumcision.

4. The covenant with Moses. Ex. 6: 6–8, 20: 2. Deut. 7: 8, 9: 26.

God promises to redeem Israel out of Egypt which is a picture of the land of bondage in which Satan lords it over an enslaved people. God requires perfect conformity to his moral law (ten commandments) from his redeemed people. Their faithfulness is required. All this points to the Gospel in which Christ redeems his people from the bondage of sin and makes them holy. Titus 2: 14.

5. The covenant with David. Ps. 89: 3, 4, 26–37, 132: 11–18. Is. 42: 1–6, 49: 8, 50: 3, 4. Matt. 3: 1. Luke 1: 32, 33. Acts 2: 30–36.

God's mercy and salvation will find embodiment in a King who will descend from David. He will be the Messiah. In his glorious person the richness, certainty and fulness of salvation find their complete expression. He will reign over his people for ever. Luke 1: 32, 33.

6. The new covenant. Gal. 3: 15, 16, 4: 4. Heb. 8: 7–13. 9: 14–28, 13: 20.

The new covenant brings the relationship of God with his redeemed people to its highest level, 'I will be your God, and you shall be my people.' Christ by the shedding of his blood secures the salvation of his people. All that is prefigured in the previous covenants is fulfilled in him. Covenant grace foretold by Jeremiah, 31: 31–34, and Ezekiel 36: 25–38, finds its zenith in the union of believing sinners with Christ. The promise that the Jews as a nation will experience the new covenant is inescapable. 'I will put my spirit within you and ye shall dwell in the land that I gave to your fathers; and ye shall be my people, and I will be your God.' Ez. 36: 27, 28.

2. The implication of the covenant: I will take away their sins

To speak in human terms, God's great problem has been the question of forgiveness. How can he justify the sinner and still himself be just? Modern materialistic man is often obsessed with how God could create the world. The creation takes up only two chapters of Genesis. The rest of the Bible is concerned with redemption, God's justification of guilty sinners on the grounds of the atonement he himself has provided.

Redemption requires the provision of a perfect righteousness and the imputation of that righteousness to sinners so that at one and the same time God is just, and the justifier of him that believes in Jesus. Rom. 3: 26.

One of the most serious weaknesses in evangelical churches today is an inadequate conception of what sin is. It includes the state of our hearts. The heart of man is evil. Out of the heart proceed all kinds of evil thoughts which lead to evil actions. Jealousy or thoughts of revenge and anger can, and sometimes do, lead to violence or murder and therefore are sinful in themselves. Sensual lust leads to adultery. This explains why Jesus said: 'Ye have heard that it was said by them of old time, Thou shalt not commit adultery: But I say unto you, That whosoever looketh on a woman to lust after her hath committed adultery with her already in his heart.' Matt. 5: 27, 28.

Sin is contrary to the nature, will and glory of God. It has degraded man and turned him into a fool. Ralph Venning, a Puritan writer, aptly titled his 288-page book defining sin as, *The Plague of Plagues*.[1] To be guilty of transgression before God is to be condemned for ever. Perhaps there is no more solemn passage in the Bible than that where Christ describes the Great Judgment in Matthew chapter 25, where he speaks of unending banishment from the presence of God which is hell.[2] We can see then what an immense thing it is for God to take away our sins.

---

1. Reprinted by *The Banner of Truth*. 30p.
2. cf. Mark 9: 42–50.

This removal of sin is referred to in graphic ways in the Scriptures. It is described as *remission* of sins. Remission means *the sending away* of something. In Leviticus, chapter 16, we are given an account of the high priest laying his hands on the head of a goat. This symbolized the imputing of the transgressions of the people to the goat. The animal was then carried by a fit man into the wilderness and there freed to disappear for ever. In the meantime another goat was sacrificed. On the grounds of that sacrifice the sins of the people were sent away into the wilderness. That is remission – our sins are sent away for ever.

Isaiah uses the term 'blotted out'. That your sins may be 'blotted out' or annihilated. Is. 43: 25. If you feel the guilt of sin weighing upon your conscience, consider the invitation of God through Isaiah, 'Come now, let us reason together, saith the Lord, though your sins be as scarlet, they shall be as white as snow: though they be red like crimson, they shall be as wool.' Is. 1: 18. Clearly that means the taking away of your sins. Micah calls it the casting away of our sins into the depths of the sea. Mic. 7: 19. Can there be a more important question for any person to consider than this: have my sins been taken away?

3. To whom this is applied: *with them,* when I take away *their* sins

We come now to the question of whether this taking away of sins applied only to a small remnant of Israelites who believed on Jesus when he came into this world, or whether this taking away of sins applies to the nation as a whole. I have shown that the apostle is speaking to ethnic Israel throughout the context. Verse 27 is no exception. Paul is appealing to the Old Testament to substantiate his assertion that 'all Israel shall be saved.'

'As it is written' he says, appealing to the prophets, 'The Deliverer shall come – for this is my covenant with them, when I shall take away their sins.'

The apostle was quite sure in his own mind as to what the prophets meant in their writings at those points to which he makes appeal. They predicted a time when Israel *as a body* would be saved. Their sins would be taken away.

Paul's appeal to Jeremiah, 31 : 34, 'I will remember their sin no more' and Isaiah, 59 : 20, 'The Redeemer shall come to Zion, and unto them that turn from transgression in Jacob,' teaches us three things. Firstly it provides an invaluable key to interpretation of the contexts to which he appeals. Secondly it shows us how he understood the verses which he quotes. Thirdly we see that by comparing New Testament appeals to their Old Testament settings we increase our understanding of both.

In application of these principles to Jer. 31 : 34 we learn that the very marrow of the covenant, in its fullest and highest expression, is to be applied to the nation of Israel as a whole in the future. Note that the entire context applies to Israel: 'Behold, the days come, saith the Lord, that I will make a new covenant with the house of Israel, and with the house of Judah: not according to the covenant that I made with their fathers in the day that I took them by the hand to bring them out of the land of Egypt; which my covenant they brake, although I was an husband unto them, saith the Lord: but this shall be the covenant that I will make with the house of Israel; After those days, saith the Lord, I will put my law in their inward parts, and write it in their hearts; and will be their God, and they shall be my people. And they shall teach no more every man his neighbour, and every man his brother, saying, Know the Lord: for they shall all know me, from the least of them unto the greatest of them, said the Lord:

for I will forgive their iniquity, and I will remember their sin no more.' Jer. 31 : 31–34.

Having established that by 'all Israel' the apostle means ethnic Israel; that the whole context of Rom. 11 concerns ethnic Israel; that their calling is without repentance and that God has promised to take away their sins, we are now in a position to answer further questions such as, *how* will Israel be converted?

HOW WILL ISRAEL BE CONVERTED?

'There shall come out of Zion the Deliverer:
He shall turn away ungodliness from Jacob.' Romans 11: 26.

At first sight the conversion of large numbers of Jews seems
very unlikely. The Jews are still contemptuous of Christ's
witness to be God's only Son, their promised Messiah.
Large numbers are agnostic, materialistic, ungodly, or
even profane. Others are implacably orthodox and reject
the New Testament with inflexible dogmatism. Is it not
vain to attempt their conversion? Paul's reply is steadfast:
'God is able to graft them in again.' Verse 23. He is able to
graft them in through *the* Deliverer. Who is this Deliverer?

1. The Deliverer – the Lord Jesus Christ

Only the one true God can forgive sin and he only, the
sovereign creator of the universe, can free a man from the
love of sin. Jesus Christ, as his name suggests, can do both
these things. He is *the Christ*, meaning *God's anointed one*,
who has authority to remove the guilt of sin. He can forgive
on the grounds of his own perfect sacrifice for sins upon
the Cross for ever. Heb. 10: 14. His name is called *Jesus*,
meaning *Saviour*, because he has spiritual power to extricate
men and women from the slavery of sin.

The great deliverer of the Old Testament was Moses.
He was the grand type of the deliverer to come. Moses
freed Israel from the slavery of Egypt foreshadowing Christ
who delivers his people from the dominion of sin. And it is
Christ alone who can turn away ungodliness from Jacob –
the name sometimes used for the Jewish people.[1]

---

1. cf. Ex. 19: 3, Luke 1: 33.

A glance at the nature of Christ, our deliverer, will show that he alone is able to convert the Jews. The New Testament reveals Jesus Christ to be the only begotten Son of God, the only mediator between God and man, great high priest, and King. He is also head and saviour of the Church, the heir of all things, and judge of the world.[1] The saviour of the New Testament alone fulfils all the descriptions ascribed to the Messiah in The Old Testament. He is unique. He is the child born, called, 'Wonderful, Counsellor, The Mighty God, The Everlasting Father, The Prince of Peace.' Is. 9: 6. This Son of God, the second person of the Trinity is equal with the Father and *is* the Deliverer of whom the text speaks.

2. The Deliverer will come out of Zion. Verse 26[2]

Whether we interpret the words Zion or Jerusalem, literally or figuratively depends in each case upon the context. Romans chapter 11 in entirety refers, as we have seen, to a comparison between the Gentiles and Israel. However Zion, the physical Zion, the mountain upon which Jerusalem is built, is obviously not part of the sustained contrast between Jews and Gentiles in Paul's reasoning. Zion therefore should be taken here in the figurative or symbolical sense.

Reference to the Old Testament will confirm this claim. Whereas Jerusalem and Israel are almost always used in the literal sense, Zion in the Old Testament is invariably employed as a symbol of *God's people*. We have for instance Ps. 2: 6. 'I have set my king upon my holy hill of *Zion*.' Jesus is not merely king over a pile of stones! He is king over the spiritual building called the Church. Eph. 2: 20-22.

---

1. John 3:16, I Tim. 2: 15, Heb. 5: 5, 6, Luke 1: 33, Eph. 5: 23, Heb. 1: 2, Acts 17: 31.
2. See Appendix I for further details.

The word 'Zion' is used in Ps. 102: 16. 'When the Lord shall build up *Zion*, he shall appear in his glory.' The reference here is certainly to building the Church and not to physical building. Christ is magnified in every revival of Christianity. Hence the expression 'he shall appear in his glory'. Other examples in which the word *Zion* is used in a spiritual sense are Ps. 110: 2. 'The Lord shall send the rod of thy strength out of the midst of Zion: rule thou in the midst of thine enemies.' Jehovah speaks to Christ and promises him that spiritual power will be exercised through the Church so that sinners will be converted. Also Is. 66: 8 which declares that as soon as Zion (the Church) travailed she brought forth her children; that is she multiplied in numbers.[1]

3. The Deliverer will not come physically to Jerusalem

Literal interpretation of the book of Revelation is one reason for the widespread belief that Jesus will return to earth and reign in Jerusalem for a thousand years. The prevalence of this idea is harmful since apart from other factors it encourages the feeling that there is little Christians can do until Christ comes to reign on earth. Refutation of this serious error is necessary.

It should be noted at the outset that apart from a reference in Peter, II Pet. 3: 8, the only mention of a thousand years in the New Testament is in Revelation. Rev. 20: 4. Hard and fast beliefs based on a highly figurative chapter are precarious indeed. Moreover, there are strong reasons for rejection of the whole idea of a physical reign of Jesus on earth for a thousand years. This theory is at variance with the fact that this present final age is the era of the Holy Spirit.

---

1. cf. Ps. 126: 1 and 134: 3.

In an extended passage recorded in the gospel of John, chapters 13–17, our Lord prepared his disciples for his departure into heaven. He tells them that it is to their advantage that he goes away. If he does not leave them, the Holy Spirit will not come. When *he*, the Comforter, comes, *he* will convince the world of sin, of righteousness and judgment to come. The Holy Spirit will lead believers into all truth and glorify Christ. John 16: 7–15.

The Bible teaches us that each person of the Trinity has a part in the salvation of men. The Father plans and directs everything. It is he who chose believers before the world began. The Son, Jesus Christ, died for us. His great work was to lay down his life for us as a substitutionary, vicarious atonement for sin. The Holy Spirit applies the meritorious work of Christ to believers. He draws sinners, regenerates them, gives them repentance and faith, teaches them, sanctifies them, and preserves them in faith to the end.

The physical presence of Christ on earth is not necessary for this work. Men and women by nature are not spiritually regenerated by witnessing the supernatural and there is no reason to suppose that a moral change would automatically take place if men saw the face of Christ. Sensational events impress men, arouse their curiosity, but have no power to renew them. 'If one rose from the dead,' said Jesus, 'you would not believe.' The reason why Christ has returned to the Father is that he might send the Holy Spirit. John 14: 16–26. In the meantime the Lord is preparing our eternal home for us. John 14: 1–3. He makes no mention whatever of an interim provision for believers to live on earth with him at Jerusalem.

Jesus disdained the idea that we should cling to his bodily presence. His physical presence affords no special advantage. It inverts the Divine order concerning the respective work of the Son and Holy Spirit. Jesus will stay at the Father's right hand and will return only when the whole work of redemption is complete. When his enemies have become his footstool he will return to end this world.[1] He never hinted at any personal physical reign on earth. Rather, the whole weight of Scripture leads us to believe that he will appear a second time without sin to salvation. With this second coming the scripture links the final day of the resurrection of the just and unjust, the great judgment, and the end of the world. No thousand-year period can be squeezed in between these events.[2] Jesus has promised to be with us until the end of the world through the Holy Spirit. 'Lo I am with you alway, even unto the end of the world.' Not until then will we see him. When we do, we will be like him and have transformed, glorified bodies.

4. How the Deliverer, through Zion, will revive Israel

There are a number of Scriptures, such as Ez. 37, Jer. 32, Is. 11 and 49 and Zech. 12, 13, which many take as describing the gathering again of the Israelites during the time which stretches from the first advent of Christ to his second coming which period is described in the New Testament as 'the last days'. Acts 2: 17, I John 2: 18, II Tim. 3: 1. Of the prophecies just quoted the one from

---

1. Ps. 110: 1, 2, I Cor. 15: 25, Heb. 1: 13, 10: 12, 13.
2. B. B. Warfield expounds upon the unity of the last events in *Biblical and Theological Studies*. He shows with clarity that when Jesus comes again it will be to end and judge the world. pp. 463–502. cf. *Systematic Theology*, A. H. Strong, p. 1011. The last events: Christ's Coming, The Resurrection, End of the World and Judgment (Matt. 25, II Thess. 1, II Peter 3) are one, none of which is to be separated by 1,000 years. There are not two second comings of Christ with Christ going up and down from Jerusalem over and over again. Some have disrupted the unity of the last events by misinterpretation of the highly figurative Rev. 20 passage. Hence whole schemes of prophecy and lorry-loads of books rest on sinking sand! See Appendix A.

Zechariah is particularly enlightening since it describes a revival. That this revival refers to the Jews of a future age is indicated by the context. Zechariah, among the last of the Old Testament prophets, prophesies events concerning the coming Grecian conqueror, Alexander, chapter 9: 9, 10 and describes the Maccabean deliverances, chapter 9: 11–17. Following this he refers to Christ, chapter 11: 1–14, and describes the curse which will follow the rejection of the Messiah, Chapter 11: 15–17. From chapter 12: 1 to 13: 6 he speaks of future blessings for Israel, God's protection of her against surrounding nations, and of her repentance and reformation.

The revival described in chapter 12: 8–14, has all the characteristics of every Holy Spirit revival since Pentecost. Of this section T. V. Moore declares: 'This chapter refers to a great revival of religion in the Church, which is as yet future, and to this revival especially as it should include the Jews, who would at that time be restored to the Church from which they had for so long been separated by unbelief. The depth of their penitence is described very vividly in chapter 12: 8–14. Connected with this penitence, however, there would be what their previous mourning had never obtained, a full possession of pardon. This is represented by the metaphor of a fountain, that bestows the double blessing of refreshment to the thirsty and purification to the unclean.'[1] It would help to read the passage and then state the teaching to be drawn from it. 'And I will pour upon the house of David, and upon the inhabitants of Jerusalem, the spirit of grace and of supplication: and they shall look upon me whom they have pierced, and they shall mourn for him, as one mourneth for his only son, and shall be in bitterness for him, as one that is in bitterness for his firstborn. In that day shall

---

1. *Commentary on Zechariah*, p. 204.

there be a great mourning in Jerusalem, as the mourning of Hadadrimmon in the valley of Megiddon. And the land shall mourn, every family apart; the family of the house of David apart, and their wives apart; the family of the house of Nathan apart, and their wives apart; the family of the house of Levi apart, and their wives apart; the family of Shimei apart, and their wives apart; all the families that remain, every family apart, and their wives apart. In that day there shall be a fountain opened to the house of David and to the inhabitants of Jerusalem for sin and for uncleanness.' Zech. 12: 10–13: 1.

The following conclusions seem inescapable:

1. There shall be a glorious outpouring of the Holy Spirit upon the whole nation of Israel. The Lord Jesus Christ will send out the rod of his strength through Zion, his believing churches.

2. This outpouring of the Spirit will be characterized by the invariable marks of a revival. It will be preceded and carried on by a wave of earnest prayer. The crucified Christ will be the centre of the Holy Spirit's revelation. His atonement will be the sole source of the washing away of sin and consequent imputed righteousness. Repentance will arise from a sight of a dying Saviour.

3. The pouring out of the Spirit will be upon the whole nation and will include all levels of society. The mass of the people will be affected.

4. This outpouring of the Spirit will bring about a repentance centred in their own particular national sin of crucifying their Messiah. Simultaneous with a realization of the efficacy of his sacrifice for the cleansing of their sin will be a broken heart, a mourning that they have been guilty of the appalling sin of unbelief. Their sorrow will be heightened through a consideration of the fact that they have for so long continued in a state of obduracy.

5. This repentance produced by the Holy Spirit in the

nation will be *evangelical* in that it is centred in Christ; *deep* in that it will recognize the extent of their sin of piercing him; *bitter* in that it will be as when the whole nation lamented the tragic death of young King Josiah, or as when parents lose their only son; *universal* for the *land* will mourn. It will be *domestic*, every family mourning apart, and *personal*, wives and husbands mourning apart.

6. This repentance will lead not only to justification by faith but also to sanctification by the Spirit. Sin will be forgiven and uncleanness purged away.

Conclusion

To summarize this chapter we may say with certainty that the conversion of the Jews will come through the One who holds the keys of death and life, the exalted, reigning monarch of the universe. Moreover, it is certain that he does not need to return to earth to restore the Holy Spirit to Israel. He does not need to be physically present on earth to ingraft her into the believing Church. We can be sure that the main elements of every Holy Ghost revival will be present when the Jews are restored.

As to further details we cannot be certain. Whether this revival will be one spontaneous event or whether it will be accomplished in successive waves we cannot determine. The proportion of Jews converted is likewise unknown. Nor can we be certain as to the extent to which the Gentile Church must be revived before it pleases the Deliverer to come from her to embrace the unbelieving Jews with the saving Gospel. We know enough to pray fervently for the salvation of the Jews on a large scale.

'life from the dead'. Romans 11 : 15.

'The conversion of the Jews,' says Charles Hodge, 'will be attended with the most glorious consequences for the whole world.'[1] If there is joy among the angels in heaven over one sinner that repents then we can well imagine the feast of gladness that will take place when Israel is brought at last into God's marvellous light. Paul describes the receiving of Israel as 'life from the dead' to the Gentiles, Rom. 11 : 15.

A glorious event for the Gentiles

David Brown, eminent expositor of the last century, paraphrases verse 15 in this way: 'Now if the fall of the Israelites be the riches of the Gentile world, and the diminishing of them (or the reduction of the true Israel to so small a remnant as then believed) be the riches of the Gentiles; how much more their fulness (or full recovery)? For if the casting away of them be the reconciling of the (Gentile) world, what shall the receiving of them be (to that Gentile world) but LIFE FROM THE DEAD?'[2]

The meaning of the phrase, 'life from the dead', suggests that the receiving of the Jews who have been such inveterate rejectors of the Cross, will make an extraordinary impression upon Gentile believers. Such an act of mercy and revelation from God will undoubtedly astonish believers and rejuvenate their faith. As Patrick Fairbairn

---

1. *Romans*, p. 364.
2. *The Restoration of Israel*, p. 224.

declares, 'Were Jerusalem but effectually reached by the power of the Gospel, every nation under heaven would be stirred.'[1]

What is the state of Gentile churches in the world today? The answer is that evangelical churches generally throughout the world are in a state of weakness. There are tens of thousands of such churches but genuine spiritual revival is only rarely to be found among them. Many churches have the appearance of life. They have a name to live but are dead. Rev. 3: 1. Conviction of sin, appetite for prayer meetings, and the study of doctrine is exceptional. There is enthusiasm for Hollywood-type films, glossy easy-to-read magazines, swing groups, sermonettes, exciting campaigns, variety programmes in the services and entertainment. Spirit-filled preachers who expound the Scriptures so as to bring transformation of life to all classes of society are uncommon. Twentieth century evangelicalism bears marks of superficiality. Truths loved by our forefathers are now largely despised. Contention for them is regarded with cynicism and even ridicule.

Evangelicalism today is world-wide but is deficient in depth, in doctrine, in unity and in vital spiritual life. If spiritual life produces the resolute courage of William Tyndale, the passionate zeal of George Whitefield, the persevering faith of William Carey, and the evangelical fervour of John Wesley, then paucity of such life is all too evident. Evangelicalism instead of developing and maturing natural gifts and genius often seems to have inhibiting and repressing effects upon personalities. The life of the Spirit leads to imaginative and constructive enterprise, sterling effort and endurance. Under pressure of set-back or opposition, the life of the Spirit manifests itself in beauty of character, in meekness, humility, love, joy, peace and

---

1. *The Intep. of Prop.*, p. 265.

gentleness. The beauty and depth of the life of Jesus which the Holy Spirit produces in believers is seldom seen. The churches are in dire need of life – of 'life from the dead'.

What consequences are likely to follow the salvation of all Israel? David Brown in his *Restoration of Israel*, written a century ago, gives light on this question:

'I. Men's faith in the Biblical History, and in the reality of religion, will then seem as "life from the dead".

II. The triumphs of the Gospel thence accruing will be as "life from the dead".

III. Men's confidence in the faithfulness of God will then be as "life from the dead".'

Certainly the conversion of Israel is likely to bring about a new confidence in the Word of God, which for so long has been the target of doubt and criticism.

The extent to which the Christian churches have been strengthened by converts from Jewry is not widely realized. If enriched by a remnant how much more will be the case were a multitude to be grafted into their own olive tree?

In 1909, a Rev. A. Bernstein wrote a book titled *Some Jewish Witnesses for Christ*.[1] If this book were available today it might well serve to illustrate the point. Hundreds of lives are outlined by Bernstein from which several could be singled out as exceptional. Take Joseph Wolff, 1795–1862, as an example. He was a pioneer missionary whose explorations were on a par with those of David Livingstone. His almost superhuman efforts have been likened to those of the Apostle Paul. At one time he had to walk naked for 600 miles in India after narrowly escaping death.

---

1. 535 pp. Operative Jewish Converts Institute.

Then, to cite another example there was Dr. Alfred Edersheim. An outstanding scholar and master of seven languages, his books continue to be highly valued today. Yet another was Adolf Saphir, a powerful preacher and gifted author, who died in 1891. One more example will illustrate the blessing accruing to the church upon the addition of gifted converts from Jewry. Dr. F. C. Ewald, 1801–1873, laboured in North Africa, Jerusalem and finally in England. Of 50,000 Jews in England at that time Ewald estimated that 3,000 had been converted. He cited as many as eleven ministers in London alone, of Hebrew stock, who were preaching the Gospel of Christ to lost sinners.

(a) The earth shall be filled with knowledge. Habakkuk 2: 14

Habakkuk, like many of his fellow prophets, was called to live during times of intense discouragement. Fervent were his prayers for a revival of religion. Hab. 1: 1–4. But instead of sending revival God pronounced judgment upon Israel. Hab. 1: 5–11. This judgment was to come by the hands of the heathen Chaldeans. Habakkuk's agony was bitter. How could a holy God use so vile an instrument as the Chaldeans? Habakkuk prayed again and with indignation set himself upon a watch tower to see what God would say. Hab. 1: 12–2: 1. Jehovah did respond. He declared that his purpose of judgment upon Israel was unalterable. However, Habakkuk was to know that he would punish the Chaldeans as well. For the prophet's comfort God gave him a heartening assurance. What was it? 'For the earth shall be filled with the knowledge of the glory of the Lord, as the waters cover the sea.' Hab. 2: 14.

For Habakkuk the fig tree would not blossom, neither would fruit be in the vines. Nevertheless he was to know that the day would come when God's cause would triumph in the earth. That wonderful promise can be opened up as follows:

1. The place of God's redemption: The earth. Ps. 22: 27, 67: 2.
2. The way of God's redemption: A knowledge of the Gospel. John 17: 3.
3. The purpose of God's redemption: God's glory. John 17: 5.
4. The extent of God's redemption: The earth shall be filled with it.
5. The advance of God's redemption: As the waters cover the sea.

The figure used to describe the advance of the Gospel is vivid. If you observe a land being irrigated you might well be impressed by the gradual and thorough way in which the ground is covered with water. The limits of the sea are precisely defined. A huge but exact expanse is filled in with ocean. So, according to the figure used, the entire world will be permeated with a knowledge of the Gospel of Christ. The parallel passage, Is. 11: 9, reveals that the secondary effects of the Gospel will be present, such as peace on earth. Swords and armaments will be beaten into ploughshares: budgets for war machines will become budgets for agricultural equipment to help feed rather than mutilate a soaring world population.

(b) The stone shall become a mountain. Daniel 2: 34, 35

'Thou sawest till that a stone was cut out without hands, which smote the image upon his feet that were of iron and clay, and brake them to pieces. Then was the iron, the clay, the brass, the silver, and the gold, broken to pieces together, and become like the chaff of the summer threshing floors; and the wind carried them away, that no place was found for them: and the stone that smote the image became a great mountain and filled the whole earth.' Dan. 2: 34, 35.

Daniel was able to interpret this dream which God placed in the mind of Nebuchadnezzar, and his words are full of instruction concerning the future. The colossus described is terrifying in its proportions. The gold head represents Babylon, the silver shoulders Medo-Persia, the brass waist Greece and the iron mixed with clay the Kingdom of the Caesars. The stone, so insignificant, is not produced by human instrumentality. It is cut without hands. It comes from God. The stone symbolizes God's Son. When the fulness of time was come God sent forth his Son, made of woman, made under the law. Gal. 4: 4.

Christ, born during the reign of Caesar Augustus, Luke 2: 1, is predestinated by the Father to set up a kingdom in men's hearts which will triumph over all other kingdoms. When all the dominions of this earth are reduced to powder and blown away by the winds of time to be remembered no more, then Christ's Kingdom will stand like a great eternal temple. His Kingdom is destined to become a mountain which fills the whole earth.

(c) All nations shall call him blessed. Psalm 72: 17

Psalm 72 consists very largely of a prophecy describing the blessedness of the reign and Kingdom of Christ, the Son of David. That these foreshadowings of the glory of his Kingdom concern this present earth is seen in verse 16: 'There shall be an handful of corn in the earth upon the top of the mountains; the fruit therof shall shake like Lebanon: and they of the city shall flourish like grass of the earth.' Ps. 72: 16. The principle taught here is that there is mighty expanding power in the Gospel. How pathetic was that small band of disciples headed by a few plain fishermen when Jesus was removed from earth's scene! Yet the fruit of Pentecost shook like Lebanon. How feeble were Wycliffe and his itinerant preachers. Yet that handful of men laid the foundations of Protestantism in England and prepared a highway for the Reformation.

If revivals came today the results would defy calculation. They might best be described in the words of this Psalm: 'He shall have dominion also from sea to sea, and from the river to the ends of the earth. His enemies shall lick the dust. All kings shall fall down before him. All nations shall serve him. All nations shall call him blessed.'

(d) The parables of the mustard seed and leaven

'Then said Jesus, Unto what is the Kingdom of God like? and whereunto shall I resemble it? It is like a grain of mustard seed, which a man took, and cast into his garden; and it grew, and waxed a great tree; and the fowls of the air lodged in the branches of it. And again he said, Whereunto shall I liken the Kingdom of God? It is like leaven, which a woman took and hid in three measures of meal, till the whole was leavened.' Luke 13: 18–21.

It should be noted that the main point illustrated in both parables is that of gradual organic growth. In the parable of the mustard seed the contrast between the size of the seed and the final result is impressive. This contrast is true to the facts. The death of one man on a cross outside the city of Jerusalem was almost like tossing a microscopic seed into the wilderness to die. The seed does die, but it comes to life again and begins to grow.[1] At first it is a tiny sapling. Gradually, however, growth continues until the sapling becomes a gigantic tree.

---

1. cf. John 12: 24.

In the parable of the leaven we need not be troubled, as many have been, by the fact that leaven is sometimes used as a symbol of corruption. (The lion is also used in both good and bad senses in scripture.)

In addition to the idea of organic growth there is the concept of the power or controlling factor being inherent within the body. As in the case of the mustard tree growth takes place from within. The indispensable mark of every Christian is that he has the Holy Spirit within him. If any man has not the Spirit of Christ he is none of his. Rom. 8: 9.

The conclusion to be drawn from these two parables is that the Kingdom of God is organic, that growth takes place gradually from powers within the body, and that the end result is very large. From the parable of the mustard tree we are led to believe that the kingdom will grow into immense proportions. It began with the Jews, continued on an ever increasing scale among the Gentiles and is yet to embrace both Jews and Gentiles together.

(e) The times of restitution of all things. Acts 3: 21

After Peter healed the lame man at the Temple Gate there was great excitement – 'all the people ran together unto them in the porch that is Solomon's, greatly wondering.' Acts 3: 11.

Peter then preached a sermon to the Jews which is one of the most powerful on record. It applies to the children of Israel in particular. Peter asserts that the miracle is not his, but Christ's, and he charges them with *killing the Prince of life; whom God has raised from the dead*, verse 19. He calls them to repentance and conversion, that their sins might be blotted out, *when the times of refreshing shall come from the presence of the Lord*, verse 19. That long period of spiritual prosperity and joy of which the prophets spoke is

73

here held out to them and made to hinge upon their national conversion.

And he shall send Jesus Christ, which before was preached unto you: Whom the heaven must receive until the times of restitution of all things, which God hath spoken by the mouth of all his holy prophets since the world began, verses 20, 21.

Peter here promises that Jesus Christ who brings peace and joy unspeakable will be sent into the hearts of the Jews bringing spiritual joy and refreshment, if they turn and repent. This same Jesus who comes to all who so turn, must abide in heaven until Israel is restored according to the predictions of the prophets. The remedial and reconciling works of the Gospel, particularly those that follow the spiritual restitution of Israel, must find their fulfilment before Jesus Christ is revealed from heaven.

Peter concludes his sermon by reminding the Jews that Christ is that prophet spoken of by Moses, Deut. 18: 15, and that it is fatal for them not to heed him. He also reminds them that their own prophets had foretold the events they had been witnessing; that they are the children of the covenant, and that God had said to Abraham, 'in thy seed shall all kindreds of the earth be blessed.' Finally he holds forth to them the resurrected Christ as the one who has come to restore their happiness by turning away every one of them, *every one of them*, from iniquity.

It would appear from this sermon that Peter anticipated 'the restitution of all things' as a restitution which followed upon the spiritual restitution of Israel.

(f) The triumph of Christ over his enemies

Important truth concerning Christ's triumph is found in the great resurrection chapter of the Bible where Paul says, 'Then cometh the end, when he shall have delivered up the kingdom to God, even the Father; when he shall have put down all rule and all authority and power. For he must reign, till he hath put all enemies under his feet.' I Cor. 15: 24, 25.

It is generally conceded that the three greatest enemies of the Gospel have been, and are: 1. False Christianity; 2. Anti-Christian Government; 3. The religion of the false prophet Mahomet.

The power and nature of these anti-Christian forces has varied through the years. At present, about 30 per cent of the world's population is enslaved as far as the Gospel is concerned because of Communism or anti-Christian governments; at least 20 per cent is deceived by false systems such as the Papacy, Greek orthodoxy and Modernism, and about 15 per cent is completely shut up under the deception of the false prophet, Mahomet.

These mighty enemies must be put under the feet of Christ. He must reign at the Father's right hand until his enemies become his footstool. Ps. 110: 1. If the uttermost parts of the earth are to become his possession then these systems which impede the Gospel must be overcome. It is not suggested that they will be removed by force. These systems must be destroyed through enlightenment; through the spread of sound scriptural teaching.

Conclusion

The terms which govern the spiritual restoration of Israel indicate that this event will mark the beginning of a great Gospel movement – so much so that it is described as 'life from the dead'. It is likely, therefore, that a time will then commence in which many Scriptures will find their fulfilment. Whether this period will be followed by a falling away is not germane to the passage in Romans, but in this connection, it might be said that at least there will be something to fall away from. The claim made by some,[1] however, might very well be correct, that the period of decline which followed the magnificent beginning of the apostolic era can accurately be described as 'a falling away'.

Many who are opposed to the idea of a period of spiritual prosperity on earth deride the concept by caricatures of prevailing world-wide luxury and ease. This, they say, is alien to 'a narrow gate', 'few being chosen', *enduring* to the end' and 'the world lying in the hands of the wicked one'.

It ought to be remembered, however, that there is no victory for the Gospel without the greatest toil and sacrifice. God accomplishes his purposes through frail human instrumentality. Enormous effort is required in 'teaching all nations'. And when there is success the struggle against the world, the flesh and the devil continues unabated.

It would be a generous estimate to venture that one per cent of the world's population is regenerate today. My own estimate is that the proportion of evangelical Christians in the world is approximately the equivalent of the Jews. If this number rose five or ten times the effect would be tremendous. The exposition of the preceding pages need not imply anything greater than just that.

---

1. Before the second advent, which will come unexpectedly, 'The apostasy of the Jews must be completed, and the persecuting power of the Roman state be revealed.' B. B. Warfield. *Bibli. and Theol. Studies*, p. 475.

WHEN WILL ISRAEL BE CONVERTED?

II

'When the fulness of the Gentiles be come in.' Romans 11 : 25.

The blindness of the Jews as we have seen will terminate. The time marking the removal of this blindness (the removal by the Lord of the veil that lies upon their hearts, II Cor. 3: 16)[1] is described as arriving when 'the fulness of the Gentiles be come in.'

The word 'fulness' (plerōma) is used in different ways in the New Testament. It means that with which anything is filled. Of his *fulness* have all we received'. John 1 : 16. It also means the supplement of anything; the remaining part. Eph. 1: 23. The word does not have to be interpreted in the same way wherever it is used in the New Testament. The context must decide the issue in each case. For instance in verse 12 of the eleventh chapter Paul reasons that if the fall or diminishing of the Jews resulted in blessing for the Gentiles how much will *their fulness* bring surpassingly greater riches to the Gentiles.[2] The *fulness*

---

1. Albert Barnes expounds the phrase 'the veil shall be taken away' as follows: 1. The time will come when the Jews shall be converted to Christianity: expressed here by their turning unto the Lord, that is, the Lord Jesus. 2. It seems to be implied that their conversion will be a conversion of *the people* at large; a conversion that shall be nearly simultaneous; a conversion *en masse*. Such a conversion we have reason to anticipate of the Jewish nation. 3. The effect of this will be to make them acquainted with the true sense of their own scriptures, and the light and beauty of the sayings of their own prophets. Now they are in deep darkness on the subject; then they will see how entirely they meet and harmonize in the Lord Jesus. 4. The true and only way of having a correct and full meaning of the Bible is by turning to God. Love to Him, and a disposition to do His will, is the best means of interpreting the Bible.
2. Robert Haldane declares that this *fulness* of the Jews will result 'in a calling of the nations to an extent beyond anything yet witnessed, and also with a great enlargement of their knowledge of the Gospel.' *Romans*, p. 533.

spoken of here means the full complement as compared with a remnant.

When we come to verse 25 how are we to interpret the meaning of the 'fulness of the Gentiles'? The question is important because, as already indicated, the answer provides us with the key as to when the Jews will acknowledge their redeemer. 'Fulness' in verse 25 cannot mean the full complement of Gentile believers since proportionately far greater numbers are to be saved when the Jews are converted. 'Fulness' then must be limited by the fact that the full complement of Gentiles will come in at a later stage. This 'fulness', therefore, must mean the full complement of Gentiles to be saved during the time stretching from Pentecost until the spiritual restoration of Israel. Elnathan Parr is helpful at this point:

> 'Fulness of the Gentiles: A full and plentiful propagation of the Gospel, whereby many of all nations shall be converted to God.'
> Question: Is this fulness past or to come?
> – I take it that this fulness is to come; and that the Gentiles shall more zealously profess the Gospel than heretofore. My reason, first, because the faith of the Gentiles shall provoke the Jews, verse 11. Secondly, if it were come, the Jews would cease to be obstinate and blind: but yet they are as obstinate and blind as ever.

Elnathan Parr was right to think that the 'Gentiles shall more zealously profess the Gospel than heretofore.' Since his day there has been a propagation of the Gospel on a scale immeasurably greater than anything he knew in his day. If we compare what exists now with what existed during apostolic times or during the seventeenth century when Parr lived, we must admit to a Gentile fulness, at least in the following respects.

(i) A numerical 'fulness' has taken place in several nations

Since the time of the Reformation successive outpourings of the Holy Spirit upon the preached Word have led to the accession of millions of Gentile believers to the Kingdom of God in several countries. This is true of Scotland, England, Wales, Holland, Germany and Scandinavia. These awakenings as well as revivals in the United States have led, particularly during the last two hundred years, to world-wide missionary endeavour. We now think in terms of multitudes of converts in countries such as Indonesia, Korea, Taiwan, Chile, Brazil, and more recently New Guinea. Moreover, countries such as South Africa, Australia, New Zealand and Canada contain hundreds of well-established evangelical churches. These churches have contributed on a large scale to missionary expansion. Were the combined results of all this work to be compiled the result, in terms of numbers converted, would be very considerable.

(ii) A numerical 'fulness' has taken place in terms of the number of nations reached with the Gospel

The opening up to the Gospel of Africa, South America and Asia has taken place quite rapidly when we think of the long centuries during which these enormous areas lay in darkness. Travel has been facilitated by the construction of highways and roads penetrating the interior regions of vast areas. The most remote hinterland can now be reached quickly by air travel. Medical, agricultural and scientific knowledge is permeating large areas. Cities which now contain millions have mushroomed within a hundred years. Parallel with these developments has been the spread of the Gospel. A Baptist minister like myself, a hundred and fifty years ago, in 1798 would possibly have completed his public prayer for Baptist missionaries at Sunday morning service with one sentence. 'Lord, protect and prosper William Carey.' Now if we have to remember all the different missionaries and varied missionary interests by name it might take many hours to complete. We are living in a time when the Gospel is being heralded to every nation, tribe and kindred under the sun.

(iii) A numerical 'fulness' has been achieved in regard to the translation of the Bible

Some part of the Scriptures is now available to men in about 1,300 languages. About 98 per cent of the world's literate population is now able to obtain the Scriptures in a language they can understand. Some countries have a very high literacy rate such as Japan with 99·8 per cent. Apart from relatively small Indian tribal groups the whole continent of South America speaks either Spanish or Portuguese. This greatly facilitates the propagation of Bibles and Christian literature. Africa remains one of the difficult continents regarding the spread of Scriptures due to wide diversity of language and low literacy rates. Only 25 per cent of the population of 55 million in Nigeria is literate. Eighty different languages are spoken in the Congo but since 1956 over six million copies of Scripture have been distributed in fifty different languages among the 14 million inhabitants of the Congo Basin.[1]

These sample references serve to give some idea of the 'fulness' that has taken place in regard to the translation and distribution of the Scriptures throughout the world.

---

1. Annual reports abounding with facts and figures are produced by *The British and Foreign Bible Society*. *The Trinitarian Bible Society*, and *Scripture Gift Mission* also furnish factual reports concerning the distribution of the Scriptures throughout the world. An excellent survey of the world scene is provided in Leslie Lyall's *Missionary Opportunity Today*, I.V.F., 25p.

2. The 'fulness of the Gentiles' – a reference to time

'Blindness', writes Paul, 'is happened to the Jews *until* the fulness of the Gentiles be come in.' The blindness of the Jews has a terminus in the calendar. Our Lord refers to the end of Jewish desolation as follows: 'O Jerusalem, Jerusalem, which killest the prophets, and stonest them that are sent unto thee; how often would I have gathered thy children together, as a hen doth gather her brood under her wings, and ye would not!

'Behold, your house is left unto you desolate: *and verily I say unto you, Ye shall not see me, until the time come when ye shall say, Blessed is he that cometh in the name of the Lord.*' Luke 13: 34, 35. cf. Matthew 23: 37–39.

When the veil is taken from their hearts the Israelites will bless the messengers of the Gospel who come in the name of the Lord Jesus.

Perhaps the most important reference in regard to the termination of Jewish blindness and the completion of the times of the Gentiles is found in Luke's record of the Olivet discourse: 'And they shall fall by the edge of the sword, and shall be led away captive into all nations: and Jerusalem shall be trodden down of the Gentiles, until the times of the Gentiles be fulfilled.' Luke 21: 24.[1]

A spiritual interpretation is sometimes required of the City of Jerusalem as for instance in the case of David's passage; 'The Lord shall bless thee out of Zion: and thou

---

1. David Brown on 'Jerusalem shall be trodden down of the Gentiles until –' declares: '1. That one day Jerusalem shall cease to be "trodden down by the Gentiles". Rev. 11: 2, as then by pagan so now by Mohammedan unbeliever; 2. That this shall be at "the completion" of "the times of the Gentiles", which from Rom. 11: 25 (taken from this) we conclude to mean till the Gentiles have had their *full time* of that place in the Church which the Jews in *their time* had before them – after which, the Jews being again "grafted into their own olive tree", one Church of Jew and Gentile together shall fill the earth. Rom. 11. What a vista this opens up!'

shalt see the good of Jerusalem all the days of thy life.'
Ps. 128: 5. In the Olivet discourse, however, it is clear that
our Lord is describing the literal end of that city as well.
It will be utterly destroyed. Not one stone will be left
upon another. Luke 21: 5. And 'Jerusalem will be trodden
down of the Gentiles *until* the times of the Gentiles be
fulfilled.' Verse 24. Here physical Jerusalem is in view.
The time of her Gentile domination will end when the
times of the Gentiles are fulfilled, Rom. 11: 25.

Conclusion

In A.D. 70 Jerusalem was literally trodden down of the
Gentiles. June 1967, marked the time when this Gentile
domination over the old city terminated.[1] Does this phrase
'the times of the Gentiles' used by our Lord coincide with
the expression used by Paul in Rom. 11: 25: 'until the
fulness of the Gentiles be come in'? The first is a reference
to time, and the second to an era when salvation is confined for the most part to the Gentiles. There seems little
to discourage the view that the end of Gentile domination
over Jerusalem is the time signal that the times of the
Gentiles are now ending. Therefore we should pray for,
work for, and expect our endeavours to proclaim the
Gospel to the Jews to meet with success.

---

1. See Chapter 17, in which recent events can be judged against the background of Jerusalem's history.

THE TERRITORIAL RESTORATION OF ISRAEL

12

'The Jewish people have had to fight unceasingly to keep themselves alive,' said Israel's Premier Levi Eshkol. 'Hopeful ever of redemption, we laboured to return to the land of our fathers and to set foundations for the resurgence of an exiled folk. We made an arduous way to the shores of that land. We fought to open its gates to our brethren. We acted from an instinct to save the soul of a people.'[1]

1967 marked the fiftieth anniversary of Middle East tension since the Balfour Declaration of 1917 advocated the establishment in Palestine of 'a Jewish national home'. 1967 also saw what may well be the pinnacle of that tension in the Six-day war – one of the most dramatic conflicts in history.

At the end of the war Israel found herself in control of all Jordan west of the Jordan river, a strategic strip of Syria to the north of Galilee, the whole of the Sinai peninsula up to Suez and most important of all – the Old City of Jerusalem.

Noteworthy is the connection uniformly described throughout the history of the Jews between *spiritual defection* and *national dispersion*; between *spiritual reconciliation* and *territorial restoration*. From the first dawn of their history when the covenant was made with Abraham, the Israelites were promised a land. In this land they were eventually settled as a nation. From the beginning, God warned them that defection would result in being driven from that land. Deut. 31: 32. This warning which came to Moses was

---

1. *Time*, 9 June 1967.

implicitly confirmed by Solomon. II Chron. 6: 36–38. When they were unfaithful God was patient with them but eventually he punished them by allowing them to be carried away in captivity to Babylon. Later their territorial restoration was partially accomplished together with spiritual reconciliation under Nehemiah and the post-exilic prophets.

The place given to the land of Canaan is never lost sight of in the history of the Jews. Even today it cannot be denied that the attention of the whole world has been directed towards the Jews because of their physical presence of the land of promise. Their occupation at this time in the land of their fathers is not only a cardinal subject of debate in the assembly halls of the United Nations; it is *the* bone of contention throughout the Arab world and the talking point of peoples everywhere. Moreover, every patriotic Jew is acutely conscious of the conflict being waged over his fatherland, while the Arab nations continue to vociferate against Israel, denying her right to exist. The Syrian radio and television stations remain as virulent as ever.[1] President Nasser had declared that another war with Israel is inevitable and that Egypt's forces are now training day and night.[2] Since Nasser's decease the position does not seem to have become less ominous. It is reported that Russia has strengthened Egyptian forces to an enormous extent virtually taking over her air force. *The Times*, 30 March 1971.

Let us now trace out the place accorded to the Land of Canaan in the history of the Jews.

---

1. *The Listener*, February 1968. Article by Dan Jacobson on mass media in the Middle East.
2. *The Times*, 30 April 1968.

1. God's promises to Abraham and Jacob concerning the land

To Abraham God makes several promises as follows: 'I will make thee exceeding fruitful, and I will make nations of thee, and kings shall come out of thee and I will establish my covenant between me and thee and thy seed after thee in their generations for an everlasting covenant, to be a God unto thee, and to thy seed after thee and I will give unto thee and to thy seed after thee, the land wherein thou art a stranger, all the land of Canaan, for an everlasting possession; and I will be their God.' Gen. 17: 6–8.

Note that it is declared that Abraham's seed, his physical descendants, will inherit all the land of Canaan for an everlasting possession. Moreover, he will be their personal God which may well suggest that the new covenant blessing of inward spiritual union with Christ, Heb. 8: 10, is eventually to come to them as a people.

To Jacob, the third trustee (the second being Isaac) of Abraham's covenant, God confirms these promises 'and he dreamed, and behold a ladder set up on the earth, and the top of it reached to heaven: and behold the angels of God ascending and descending on it. And, behold, the Lord stood above it, and said, I am the Lord God of Abraham thy father, and the God of Isaac: the land whereon thou liest, to thee will I give it, and to thy seed; and thy seed shall be as the dust of the earth, and thou shalt spread abroad to the west, and to the east, and to the north, and to the south: and in thee and in thy seed shall all families of the earth be blessed.' Gen. 28: 12–14.

The first promise to be confirmed is that the land upon which Jacob is lying will be given to his seed. Through his seed all nations of the earth are to be blessed which is in process of being accomplished through the

Gospel of Christ and his apostles. Finally, he is assured that he personally will be brought back into the land of Canaan. Note that the place given to *the land* is prominent.

2. God's promises to Moses pertaining to the land

In Deuteronomy Moses wrote these words: 'Rejoice, O ye nations, with his people: for he will avenge the blood of his servants, and will render vengeance to his adversaries, and will be merciful unto his land, and to his people.' Deut. 32: 43.

This verse is quoted by Paul in Rom. 15: 10 to prove the union of the believing Jews and Gentiles in Christ. The expression with which this song of praise concludes is significant, 'He will be merciful to his land, and to his people.' What people? Surely these are the same people who are explicitly distinguished from the Gentiles in the first part of the verse. What land? Surely this is the same land with which God's ancient people have always been identified.

Three points in this verse are noteworthy: 1. The Gentile nations are commanded to rejoice with the Jews. 2. God's ancient covenant people are those to whom He will show mercy. 3. Canaan is the land which God has given for an everlasting possession to his people. These three truths are inseparable. Current events in Israel compel us to think carefully of them.

In the same context of Romans fifteen Paul also quotes Is. 11: 10: 'And again, Esaias saith, There shall be a root of Jesse, and he that shall rise to reign over the Gentiles; in him shall the Gentiles trust.' Rom. 15: 12.

This reference taken from Isaiah shows that Isaiah was prophesying concerning these last times. Examination of Isaiah eleven confirms this, which passage we shall now examine.

3. God's words through Isaiah concerning the land

'And it shall come to pass in that day, that the Lord shall set his hand again the second time to recover the remnant of his people, which shall be left, from Assyria, and from Egypt, and from Pathros, and from Cush, and from Elam, and from Shinar, and from Hamath, and from the islands of the sea. And he shall set up an ensign for the nations, and shall assemble the outcasts of Israel, and gather together the dispersed of Judah from the four corners of the earth. The envy of Ephraim shall depart, and the adversaries of Judah shall be cut off: Ephraim shall not envy Judah, and Judah shall not vex Ephraim. But they shall fly upon the shoulders of the Philistines toward the west; they shall spoil them of the east together: they shall lay their hand upon Edom and Moab; and the children of Ammon shall obey them. And the Lord shall utterly destroy the tongue of the Egyptian sea; and with his mighty wind shall he shake his hand over the river, and shall smite it in the seven streams, and make men go over dryshod. And there shall be an highway for the remnant of his people, which shall be left, from Assyria; like as it was to Israel in the day that he came up out of the land of Egypt.' Is. 11: 11–16.

In Isaiah's day there was no such wide dispersion as is described above. This is one reason why it is unsatisfactory to stop with a spiritual interpretation of the passage. Isaiah predicts events of a future time, the diaspora he describes being universal in its extent. God is going to stretch out his hand to gather these, his people, from the four corners of the earth.

The following interpretation seems to do justice to Isaiah's words: The tragic divisions among the Jews which have served to destroy and weaken them will be healed in that day. They will be welded together as a united people. They shall fly upon, or assault the Philistines towards the west, and plunder or spoil their enemies in the east. Edom, Moab, and Ammon, Arab nations, have always been the inveterate enemies of Israel. There will be a reversal in the fortunes of the Israelis. Whereas they have been divided and dispersed, now they will be united and brought together. Whereas they suffered constant humiliation and defeat before, now they will be victorious over their enemies, both to the west and to the east.

The secret of their success is not natural prowess or superior intelligence or numerical advantage. The key to their re-establishment is the Lord who is merciful and who remembers his covenant with them. The tongue of the Egyptian sea is a reference to the Red Sea which once threatened to be the means of destruction to the Israelites escaping from Pharaoh but which, in fact, God divided for them. The same sea which saved Israel destroyed the Egyptians. In this context it may well symbolize the threat of Israel's enemies which God will over-rule and restrain.

The reference is not to the Babylonian exile but to a mighty future deliverance of the Israelites, reminiscent of that deliverance which he gave them when they came out of Egypt under Moses. While no direct reference is made in the passage to the locality of Canaan it is obvious that this is implied. To what other place would God gather the outcasts of Israel, and the dispersed of Judah?

4. God's word through Jeremiah concerning the land

Restoration for Israel which is yet future is indicated in Jeremiah. 'Behold, the days come, saith the Lord, that I will raise unto David a righteous Branch, and a King shall reign and prosper, and shall execute judgment and justice in the earth. In his days Judah shall be saved, and Israel shall dwell safely: and this is his name whereby he shall be called, THE LORD OUR RIGHTEOUSNESS. Therefore, behold, the days come, saith the Lord, that they shall no more say, The Lord liveth, which brought up the children of Israel out of the land of Egypt; but, The Lord liveth, which brought up and which led the seed of the house of Israel out of the north country, and from all countries whither I had driven them; and they shall dwell in their own land.' Jer. 23: 5–8.

It is difficult to maintain that the first part of this prophecy refers to Christ and the latter to the return of the Jews from Babylon. The whole passage refers rather to Gospel times when Jesus shall reign with power from the right hand of the Father. Then shall Judah be saved and Israel shall dwell safely. The Lord who will be the righteousness of both believing Jews and Gentiles will gather his ancient people from all countries whither he had driven them. Then they shall dwell in *their own land*.

5. God's Word through Ezekiel concerning the land

The whole of Ezekiel chapter 37 – the vision of dry bones – is important. One of the most exciting passages in the Bible, it lends itself to many valuable spiritual applications and lessons. But it is difficult to deny that its primary interpretation concerns the future restoration of Israel. Like other prophetic passages, especially those in Isaiah, this chapter is teleological; it points to more than one era in the future.[1] Its immediate purpose was undoubtedly to

---

1. Some theologians use the term *teleological* to describe prophecies which were designed to cast light and meaning on more than one event in the future. For discussion of principles involved see Patrick Fairbairn's *The Typology of Scripture*, Vol. 1., ch. 5.

encourage the restoration from Babylon which was imminent when Ezekiel wrote. It most certainly foreshadows the time of Pentecost when multitudes were raised from the valley of dead bones. But the graphic and precise terms employed do not find their complete fulfilment even in Pentecost. The prophecy applies to a period richer and fuller in scope than that of Pentecost. An examination of the text might bear this out:

'And say unto them, Thus saith the Lord God; Behold, I will take the children of Israel from among the heathen, whither they be gone and will gather them on every side, and bring them into their own land. And I will make them one nation in the land upon the mountains of Israel; and one king shall be king to them all: and they shall be no more two nations, neither shall they be divided into two kingdoms any more at all: Neither shall they defile themselves any more with their idols, nor with their detestable things, nor with any of their transgressions: but I will save them out of all their dwelling-places, wherein they have sinned, and will cleanse them: so shall they be my people, and I will be their God. And David my servant shall be king over them; and they all shall have one shepherd: they shall also walk in my judgments, and observe my statutes, and do them. And they shall dwell in the land that I have given unto Jacob my servant, wherein your fathers have dwelt; and they shall dwell therein even they, and their children, and their children's children, for ever: and my servant David shall be their prince for ever. Moreover I will make a covenant of peace with them; it shall be an everlasting covenant with them: and I will place them, and multiply them, and will set my sanctuary in the midst of them for evermore. My tabernacle also shall be with them: yea, I will be their God, and they shall be my people. And the heathen shall know that I the Lord do sanctify Israel, when my sanctuary shall be in the midst of them for evermore.' Ez. 37: 21–28.

If we are to do justice to this passage we must face up to the implications of a dual spiritual and territorial restoration of Israel. Not merely a remnant, but the whole body of people is to enjoy the new covenant. They will dwell in the land that God gave to Jacob his servant. The heathen will acknowledge the Lord when he arises to sanctify Israel.

Conclusion

Some argue from passages such as Deut. 4: 25–31; 28: 63–68; 30: 1–10 and Lev. 26: 33–34 that Israel's territorial restoration is wholly dependent upon national repentance. It is maintained that the present restoration is not a fulfilment of Scripture because it is entirely unspiritual. Reconciliation is the first requirement and territorial restoration the outcome: not vice-versa. This argument certainly carries weight but on the other hand we must believe that God rules the nations and nothing happens by chance. There seems to be nothing to preclude God from following the order: assembly first, conversion second. Sinners are usually brought together to hear the Word and then converted by and through that Word. Prevenient grace operates in the case of all converted people. Why should it not apply to a nation?

Christ who rules the nations with a rod of iron, Ps. 2: 6, has permitted the Jews to return to the land of their fathers. It is our duty to interpret this extraordinary providence. Why has it happened? – that they, a proud people, might suffer more through war, and by tribulation be humbled? – or is it with a purpose of mercy that Christ has permitted their return?

In conclusion let us note the connection between

reconciliation and territorial restoration. The latter, even though it is based on the precarious foundation of military conquest, is an accomplished fact. Let us pray fervently for the former, namely, the spiritual recovery of the Jews, sharing the persuasion of Greenhill so ably expressed when he wrote: "There is a time when the Jews shall not only have mercy, but abundant and lasting mercy. God will gather them, pour out his Spirit upon them, and never hide his face from them any more. This time will be a happy and glorious time. For the house of Israel to be enriched with the gifts and graces of God's Spirit, which are excellent, and to have the light of God's countenance shining upon them, and that always, what can be more desirable? This condition as Paul saith, will be 'life from the dead,' Rom. 11 : 15. Now they are like dead trees, without any sap in them; but then they will be like trees well-rooted, full of sap, and in their greatest glory; full of branches, leaves, blossoms, fruit, and the sun shining upon them."[1]

---

1. William Greenhill, (1591-1677) Exposition of Ezekiel, p. 774.

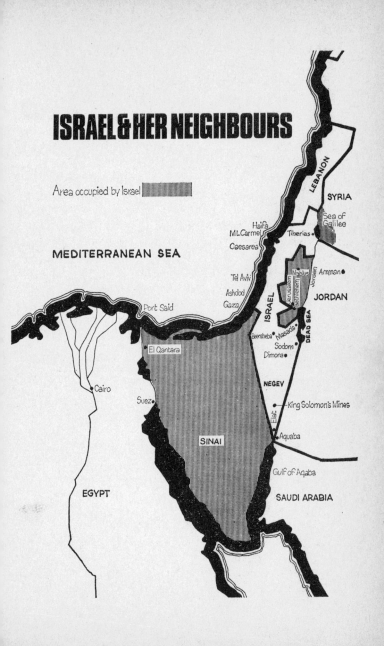

ISRAEL & HER NEIGHBOURS

Area occupied by Israel

MEDITERRANEAN SEA

LEBANON

SYRIA

Sea of Galilee

Haifa
Mt. Carmel
Caesarea

Tiberias

Tel Aviv

Ashdod
Gaza

ISRAEL

Jerusalem
Bethlehem
Nablus
Jordan

Amman

JORDAN

DEAD SEA

Port Said

Beersheba
Masada
Sodom
Dimona

El Qantara

NEGEV

Cairo

Suez

King Solomon's Mines

Elat

Aquaba

SINAI

Gulf of Aqaba

EGYPT

SAUDI ARABIA

ISRAEL – A MODERN MIRACLE

13

The word miracle is often used in a careless way. According to the Oxford dictionary a miracle is a 'marvellous event due to some supernatural agency'. This definition of the word is not exaggerated in its use when applied to events in the history of the Jews since their birth in Abraham about 3,850 years ago. Thought of in natural terms Israel should not really exist at all. Sarah was well past the age of child-bearing when God made the promise to Abraham that he would have a son. For Abraham this event required a miracle; yet he believed in the omnipotence of God. 'He staggered not at the promise but was strong in faith. Therefore there sprang even from one, and him as good as dead, so many as the stars of the sky in multitude, and as the sand which is by the sea shore innumerable.' Heb. 11: 12.

The nation was destined to increase rapidly, not through Isaac, but through the twelve sons of Jacob. Remarkable were the circumstances which brought the twelve brothers into Egypt while the events prior, and subsequent to, Joseph becoming Prime Minister bear sublime marks of Divine control and purpose.

The children of Israel passed above four hundred years in Egypt which became to them a crucible of affliction. Their increase provoked and alarmed the Pharaohs who placed them under whips and task-masters. But the more the Egyptians sought to prevent their growth by ill-devised and cruel persecution, the more they multiplied. The process escalated until life for the Jews became intolerable. Yet 'God heard their groanings'. With mighty signs and wonders, the people, now numbering about two million, were led by Moses out of Egypt. The pride of Pharaoh and the serfdom of Israel were simultaneously shattered in the miraculous exodus through the Red Sea.

The subsequent history of the Jews in which they occupied the role of God's chosen people forms the main substance of the Old Testament, a role which came to an end in their rejection of the Messiah. While they have ceased to be the subjects of God's favour, a fact evidenced both by their suffering and their failure to propagate any saving gospel to the world, they have nevertheless been preserved in a mysterious way. No other nation in history has been so persistently persecuted or dispersed: no other has experienced so unique a restoration to their former land. Both the preservation of Israel since their dispersion and their home-coming after nearly two thousand years is described as miraculous.

Terence Prittie in his recently published book, *Miracle in the Desert*[1] recounts what he regards as six separate miracles involved in this restoration which may be summarized as follows:

1. *The aliyah*, or immigration wave, into Israel was a triumph of mind over matter. Malarial swamps and sandy deserts swallowed many lives but finally surrendered to the extraordinary endurance of their conquerors. The desert has blossomed as a rose.
2. The creation of a world Zionist movement was accomplished despite violent opposition. Jewish leaders opposed the objective of the Zionist movement to create a national home in Palestine on the grounds that it was unattainable.

---

1. Pall Mall Press (1967), £2.25.

3. The Balfour Declaration of 1917 proclaiming England's disposition to favour a national home for the Jewish people in Palestine formed a vital link in the chain of events. The origins of the declaration rightly lead to the conclusion that it should be placed in the category of the extraordinary.

4. Securing co-operation from all sections of a widely diverse community speaking different languages to unite in the use of the Hebrew tongue ranks as a unique achievement.

5. The actual creation of the state of Israel in 1948, with the approval of the United Nations, was a miracle. The Jewish population in Palestine had increased from 100,000 in 1917 to about 650,000 in 1948 and mounting difficulties with the Arab population and surrounding Arab nations heightened the remarkable nature of the 1948 event.

6. The sixth miracle was the Israeli victory in the war of independence that began on 15 May 1948. Without an organized army and practically destitute of conventional military armour a small minority of ill-equipped Jews decisively defeated the armies of Egypt, Jordan, Syria, Lebanon and Iraq.

Prittie comments on these events in much more detail and mentions the seven-day war between Israel and Egypt in 1956 as an event which some might wish to classify as stupendous. He, however, chooses not to do so. Later in the same chapter he makes this comment: 'Ironically, Jewish Jerusalem overlooks the Old City, now in Jordan, and, from buildings like the Church of the Notre Dame, one has a perfect bird's-eye view of the streets of the Old City and both the Jewish and Christian Holy places. Yet, just as Israel cannot wage war to win the Jordan frontier, so, I believe, Israel cannot seek to enforce a claim to the old City.'

While the sheets upon which the above comment appeared were rolling off the press the seventh miracle was taking place and could be said to consist of the Six-day war.

On Monday, 5 June 1967, the conflict began. Friends of Israel were apprehensive about her survival. President Nasser had threatened to exterminate his Jewish neighbours, proving the sincerity of his threats with warlike actions, closing the Gulf of Aqaba to Israeli shipping, and moving up large military forces into the Gaza strip. In the meantime other Arab states such as Jordan and Syria pledged their unity with Egypt. Outnumbered by forces more than double their size in every sphere: army, navy, tanks and aircraft, the Israelis steeled themselves to win by strategy and determination.

Seldom in military history has victory been so rapid, efficient and decisive.

The story is described as one of the most remarkable military victories in the history of modern warfare. This may be so but we must guard against optimism in regard to Israel's future simply because of military triumph. Jesus said that they that take up the sword will perish by it. I am convinced, however, that the Israelis had no alternative but to defend themselves quickly and efficiently. We should also be careful not to glory in the details of war. It is the purpose of Christ to abolish bloodshed. Ps. 46: 9. Personal bereavement underlines the appalling horror of nation destroying nation. For every victim upon the battlefield or at home there are some broken hearts. Bearing these factors in mind we need only recall the main features of the Six-day war by which Israel's position was greatly altered.[1]

---

1. *The Six-day War* by Randolph S. and Winston S. Churchill, regarded by some reviewers as the best short account of the war provides all the information required by the general reader. Heinemann, 25p.

Key to the victory was the carefully planned air strike on the first day when twenty-three Arab airfields were attacked simultaneously. Flying low to avoid Egyptian radar, the Israeli pilots timed their rise into radar beams so as to provide only enough time for enemy pilots to warm their engines, so creating a perfect target for specially designed missiles. Thus in a moment, swift and terrible, planes and pilots were destroyed together. Unique Israeli designed rockets were then used to blow up enemy runways, crippling Arab retaliation.[1]

The victory on the first day was followed by others on all fronts, the war bringing about a cataclysm in the balance of power and political boundaries. When the dust settled, gains and losses were added up. Israel lost 679 men. Estimates of Arab losses vary from 10,000 to 30,000. How many Egyptian soldiers perished in Sinai may never be established. Enormous quantities of arms, including 300 undamaged tanks and intact Soviet S.A.2 ground-to-air missile units, were captured.

In proportion to her size and resources Jordan suffered the greatest losses – the destruction of her army and air force, a considerable part of her most arable land, her tourist income, and the city of Old Jerusalem. Her economy, which might have become stable by 1971, is now regarded as permanently crippled. Her refugee problem is acute.

Israel's accessions exceeded all anticipation. Apart from the oil wells of Sinai which supply twice as much fuel as Israel requires, the peninsula has strategic value providing an ideal military buffer between Israel and Egypt. Jordanian and Syrian territory has an entirely different ecology and Israel is likely to control these areas so long

---

1. Details in *Flight International*, 22 June 1967.

as the Arabs maintain their hostile attitude. Arab enmity and belligerence is the key to Israel's re-establishment. The sympathy of several nations is assured so long as the Arabs deny Israel's right to exist. And Israel will not hand back territory which will be used for military purposes in an endeavour to destroy her. The facts of Arab aggression are widely displayed. This was the case during the war and has been so subsequently. A full-page advertisement in the London *Daily Express* on 7 June 1967 provides an example. It reads: 'Israel is fighting for survival. The openly-avowed intention of the Arab nations is Israel's complete extermination – nothing less than the annihilation of two and a half million men, women and children.' The advertisement is undersigned by sixty-eight well-known personalities.

Over a hundred years ago David Brown, the commentator, expressed his certainty that[1] Israel would be territorially and spiritually restored. At that time return to the land on any realistic scale seemed an impossibility. Today Israel is a going concern. The Six-day war increased the geographical size of Israel four-fold while the Jewish population has quadrupled during the last two decades.

The last ten years has seen an eight-fold increase in mining and quarrying while the overall industrial output of the country has tripled. A million acres of land have been cultivated, more than a third of which is under irrigation. The country is almost self-supporting when it comes to foodstuffs, producing 85 per cent of her needs. She has developed a successful fishing industry of her own, 13,500 acres of fish ponds raising half her needs, and trawlers plying as far as South Africa producing much of the remainder. Investments from abroad are copious:

---

1. *The Restoration of Israel.* I discovered this little volume in the *Evangelical Library*. It had never been read as I had to cut open the pages.

contributions from Jewish communities in other countries generous. There is the bustle of tourism. Other lucrative sources of income are an increasing cotton-growing industry (35,000 acres) and the diamond-cutting business which in 1964 produced a net income of about £40,000,000.

Israel needs this prosperity in order to shoulder the heavy burden of security and defence. In addition to her own population she has the responsibility of 1,250,000 Arabs including 800,000 refugees; although it is reported that about 200,000 of these have returned to Jordan.

Fifty years' progress in restoration to their own land and the Six-day war, particularly the latter event, have served to stimulate renewed zeal among the Jews of the diaspora and revive patriotism in Israel. Israeli unity is extraordinary, especially when one considers that Jews have returned from about eighty different countries. The hatred of the Arabs and the constant round of vicious threats broadcast by radio, especially from Syria, has played no small part in creating this unity. All that has been described in this chapter concerns Israel in her natural state. What of Israel's spiritual condition? To that we now turn.

THE RESPONSIBILITY OF THE JEWS IN REJECTING CHRIST

14

In a well-documented book *Europe and the Jews* – with the sub-title – *The Pressure of Christendom on the People of Israel for 1900 years*, Malcolm Hay argues that the Jews as a people were not responsible for Christ's death. His main reason for this contention is that it was only the High Priest and his cronies who were responsible. According to Hay, John's language is supposed to be conducive to anti-semitism, whereas the synoptic Gospels make it plain that the body of Jews were not responsible at all.[1] Hay quotes Peter (in his first Papal declaration!) that the guilty Jews did it through ignorance.[2] However, according to Biblical teaching this ignorance is culpable. (cf. Paul's remarks on his own conversion, I Tim. 1 : 13).

We will now seek to prove from the Scriptures: 1. That the Jews were responsible as a people for the rejection of Christ. 2. That God's sovereignty cannot be blamed for Jewish failure, and 3. That the consequences of rejecting Christ by the Jews have continued to the present day.

1. The responsibility of the Jews in rejecting Christ

There is surely no more convincing way of proving the responsibility and guilt of the Jews than by examination of our Lord's own words. Three passages are particularly decisive; Christ's upbraiding of the Jewish cities, his lament over Jerusalem while in Galilee, and the sorrow he expressed on the occasion of his last entry into the Holy City.

---

1. See pp. 12–16.
2. ibid. p. 20.

The responsibility of the Jews is emphasized in Christ's upbraiding of the cities wherein most of his mighty works were done, *because they repented not*. They were expected to repent because they were responsible. Commensurate with their responsibility will be their punishment: 'Then began he to upbraid the cities wherein most of his mighty works were done, because they repented not: Woe unto thee, Chorazin! woe unto thee, Bethsaida! for if the mighty works, which were done in you, had been done in Tyre and Sidon, they would have repented long ago in sackcloth and ashes. But I say unto you, It shall be more tolerable for Tyre and Sidon at the day of judgment, than for you. And thou, Capernaum, which art exalted unto heaven, shalt be brought down to hell; for if the mighty works, which have been done in thee, had been done in Sodom, it would have remained until this day. But I say unto you, That it shall be more tolerable for the land of Sodom in the day of judgment, than for thee.' Matt. 11: 20–24.

Jewish responsibility is further seen in Christ's lamentations over Jerusalem. His words in the passages I quote, are so powerful and convicting that they hardly need explanation. Nevertheless to bring out the meaning with more cogency I have suggested comments in a separate column.

O Jerusalem, Jerusalem, which killest the prophets, and stonest them that are sent unto thee:

The lament of Christ underlines their responsibility. They have received so much and have produced so little repentance.

How often would I have gathered thy children together as a hen doth gather her brood under her wings, and you would not.

Christ would not attempt to gather the people unless he regarded them as fully responsible. Christ's willingness to gather the Jews and save them from impending judgment was wholehearted. As a hen is wholly concerned with gathering her chicks so Christ's fervent concern was to save those Jews. This surely stresses their responsibility.

Behold, your house is left unto you desolate:

So grave is your failure in complying with your duty that fearful judgment is to come upon you. No punishment is more severe than that of being forsaken by God.

You shall not see me, (comprehend me), until the time comes when ye shall say, Blessed is he that cometh in the name of the Lord:

This judgment is to last until the time comes when from the heart you will be able to welcome him who comes in the name of Jehovah. Judicial blindness enveloped the Jews after their rejection of Christ and will be upon them until God himself removes it. II Cor. 3: 15, 16.

The words above are recorded in Luke 13: 34, 35, while the third passage which follows is from Luke 19: 41, 42.

And Jesus, beheld the city and wept over it,

Not over bricks, stones and mortar, but over the souls of the Jews did Jesus weep. They had failed miserably to fulfil their responsibility to receive him, their Messiah. This was tragic for them and for their children.

Saying, If thou hadst known, even thou,

Of all people the Jews, who possessed the scriptures and who had been privileged with the mission of successive prophets sent from God, were to a very high degree responsible.

At least in this thy day

Had they failed to receive the prophets but at least received and embraced their messiah, amends would be made. But now, in this their greatest day of opportunity, the time of their visitation, they failed in their responsibility.

the things which belong to thy peace!

Atonement, imputed righteousness, reconciliation and the mercy of God – these things were designed by God for their eternal peace. He wished good to them but they refused and rebelled. Is. 1: 20. For their rebellion and failure God held them fully responsible.

but now they are hid from thine eyes.

Continued rejection of the truth leads to the hardening of the heart. When the heart becomes hard the mind closes. All evidence then, no matter how graciously and lucidly presented, is rejected. That is the blindness spoken of in Rom. 11: 25. *'Blindness is happened to Israel.'*

It is not then the single act of crucifying Christ that must be taken into account in determining the responsibility of the Jewish nation. The rejection of the light by the people as a whole, was the real cause which lay behind the desolation which followed. Failure to receive him was the cause, as Jesus confirmed in the words: 'For the days shall come upon thee, that thine enemies shall cast a trench about thee, and compass thee round, and keep thee in on every side, And shall lay thee even with the ground, and thy children within thee; and they shall not leave in thee one stone upon another; because thou knewest not the time of thy visitation.' Luke 19: 43, 44.

The Jews were responsible for rejecting the greatest of all God's mercies – the visitation of his dearly beloved and only begotten son. Sinless and perfect, his life proved the sincerity of his love. Jesus spoke to them 'as never man spoke'. He had compassion upon their poor. He healed their lame and their blind. He cast out demons and delivered captives from the bondage of disease and perversion.

No people since the beginning of the world enjoyed so many privileges as did the Jews. Here among them was 'God manifest in the flesh.' He tabernacled among them. John 1: 14. He came to seek and to save them. Yet they hated him without a cause. Their behaviour proves the evil of their hearts. Their malicious reasoning to slay him, proves the depravity of their minds. The perversity of their consciences is seen in their persuading themselves 'that it is good that one man die and the nation perish not'.

In the desolation that was to come upon them the Israelites had only themselves to blame. God has no pleasure in the death of the wicked but rather that the wicked should turn and live. Ez. 33: 11. How often would I have gathered you, said Jesus. God is not willing that any should perish but that all should turn and repent. II Pet. 3: 9. He desires to have all men saved. I Tim. 2: 4.

This raises problems, for it is objected that if God desires to save all men then why do we read in the Bible that he hardens them.

2. God's Sovereignty cannot be blamed for Jewish failure

'Go and tell this people, Hear ye indeed, but understand not; and see ye indeed, but perceive not,' said Jehovah to Isaiah. 'Make the heart of this people fat, and make their ears heavy, and shut their eyes; lest they see with their eyes, and hear with their ears, and understand with their heart, and convert, and be healed.' Is. 6: 9, 10.

This passage is frequently quoted by Jesus and Paul in the New Testament. What does it mean? There is a divine irony in the words. It is as though God is saying to Isaiah, 'your going to preach to these people will only prove that they are already beyond repentance. They will think that they hear and understand, but in fact their only disposition is to reject and despise the message. Your preaching will only serve to harden them more and prove beyond dispute the evil character of their hearts.' Paul's words cast light on this matter: 'For we are unto God a sweet savour of Christ, in them that are saved, and in them that perish: To the one *we are* the savour of death unto death; and to the other the savour of life unto life. And who *is* sufficient for these things?' II Cor. 2: 15, 16.

Yet in Isaiah, chapter 6, we do read of a tenth, a small remnant being saved. The blindness is not total. Although the land will be utterly desolate, yet there will be remnant according to the election of grace. If God in his great mercy chooses to overcome the obstinacy of some, and save them, despite the fact that they are as unworthy as all the rest, (as Paul confesses he was, I Tim. 1: 15) then that is pure grace. Nobody can complain. No man can arraign the justice of God. The Lord does not desire the death of the wicked. To them, as with Israel, he says, 'All day long have I stretched forth my hands unto a disobedient and gainsaying people.' Rom. 10: 21. If they perish it is not the fault of the Lord. If he does finally withdraw his spirit in an act of judicial blindness, as he has done with the Jews, then none can charge him with unfairness. He has left them to their own hearts' desires. He has left them to their own will. If he changes some of them through irresistible grace which pierces the thickest armour and melts the most stubborn heart then that is because of his unspeakable mercy.

Jehovah rose up early to send his messengers. Some they stoned and others they cast out. Finally he sent his Son. Him they took with wicked hands and slew. Still he was merciful and sent his apostles. Stephen said to them, 'ye do always resist the Holy Ghost: as your fathers did, so do ye.' Acts 7: 51, but they gnashed on him with their teeth, and stoned him. James they beheaded, thus adding to their long list of crimes. In every place they resisted the Gospel. We should not wonder at the fact that in A.D. 70, after forty years of rejecting the Gospel, their house was left them desolate. God cannot be blamed for their calamity.

3. The consequences of the rejection of Jesus by the Jews

'Your house is left unto you desolate,' said Jesus. Luke 13: 35. Once the spirit of Christ, the only mediator, was to leave their temple, their city, and their system of Judaism, nothing was left but desolation.

The rejection of Christ through unbelief led to complete spiritual ruin. Judgment came upon them which was so complete, physically and spiritually, that nothing can be compared with it. The gory annals of the blood-stained history of the human race can produce nothing to equal the siege and destruction of Jerusalem. The city was demolished. The dispersion of the Jews to all nations followed. They have suffered persecution and humiliation ever since. This act of judgment is a warning to all that there is no sin so heinous as the rejection of Christ. To reject him is to spurn God's remedy, God's mercy, God's gift and God's love. Jesus suffered untold agonies in bearing our sins. Therefore the rejection of God's Son is the greatest of all sins. It is the chief sin. 'He that believeth not shall be damned.' Mark 16: 16. Unbelief is the fountain of all sin: ungodliness the real source of all unrighteousness.

Paul writing to the Thessalonians makes the comment: 'The wrath is come upon them to the uttermost.' I Thess. 2: 16. A review of Jewish history up to modern times confirms that calamity has pursued them through the years. The words of the Jews, 'Crucify him! Crucify him! – his blood be upon us and our children,' seem charged with chilling verity.

Through the centuries the Israelites have suffered acutely. They have been persecuted by a corrupt Roman Catholic Church.[1] There have been massacres of Jews in Britain, France and Spain. As late as 15 October 1965 the Vatican began to repeal their hostile doctrines regarding the Jews. Recent persecution of the Jews includes the pogroms[2] from 1880 onwards, while this century has

---

1. Amazing documentation concerning the Pope and Hitler is to be found in *The Vatican against Europe* by Edmond Paris published by P. R. Macmillan, now distributed by the Protestant Truth Society. Memorial masses for Adolf Hitler were celebrated in May 1968 in Barcelona and Madrid, pamphlets being distributed which included the words 'for the eternal rest of Adolf Hitler'. Reported in *The Jewish Chronicle*, 17 May 1968.
2. Pogrom: organized massacre of body of people in Russia.

witnessed the fearful, almost unbelievable atrocities of the gas chambers under the Nazi régime. In the case of Auschwitz, Maidenek and Chelmo it would seem that Satan was inspiring wicked men in one last frenzied effort to annihilate the Jews. Documented works prove that 5,700,000 Jews perished under the Nazis.[1]

The annihilation of so many Jews is regarded as the greatest disaster, and by far the worst blot on the pages of human history. This catastrophe raises many questions especially in the light of Jewish responsibility. It certainly warrants separate discussion.

---

1. See bibliography for documentary information.

'The God of the Hebrew Bible is depicted as the faithful protector of his chosen people. Yet at least six million Jews died at the hands of the Nazis. To believe in the God of the Covenant today' concludes Richard L. Rubinstein, 'Jews must affirm that their creator used Adolf Hitler as the rod of his wrath to send his people to the death camps. I find myself utterly incapable of believing this. Even the existentialist leap of faith cannot resurrect this dead God after Auschwitz.'[1] Rubinstein, an American rabbi, has expressed his unbelief in a book, *After Auschwitz*. He has joined modernist theologians in asserting that God has died. Yet amazingly enough Rubinstein 'believes that religion still has a worth-while social value in an age of atheism'.[2]

Auschwitz should not destroy faith in the God of the Bible. Did not Jehovah declare that 'they provoked me to anger with their vanities' – that 'a fire is kindled in mine anger, and shall burn unto the lowest hell, – they shall be devoured with burning heat, and with bitter destruction', but also, that Jehovah 'will repent himself for his servants, when he seeth their power is gone, and there is none shut up, or left.' Deut. 32: 21–36. In the midst of wrath he will remember mercy.

Nearly three million Polish and one million Russian Jews perished together with hundreds of thousands from Czechoslovakia, Rumania and Hungary. In every country

---

1. Reported *Time* Magazine, 16 February 1968.
2. ibid.

where the Nazi conspirators gained control they sought to annihilate the Jews, including Greece, Belgium, Yugoslavia and Italy, to name a few. Denmark and Bulgaria alone were successful in protecting their Jewish populations.[1] This ghastly saga confirms many truths of Scripture, four of which can be cited as follows:

1. The truth about human depravity

Germany was the cradle of the Higher Critical Movement which affected Bible seminaries and university centres everywhere. Men were taught to regard the Bible, not as God's infallible Word to man, but as a collection of extremely fallible human documents. The Biblical idea that man is totally depraved was belittled. By 'total depravity' is meant that every part of human nature has been affected by man's falling away from God. The Bible teaches that the affections, the mind, and the will are sinful. Man's heart is estranged from God so that he does not want to think about spiritual matters. If he does think about spiritual things, his thinking is twisted and biased. Moreover, man's will is depraved. 'Ye *will not* come to me' said Jesus, 'that ye might have life.' The will, governed by the sinful lusts of the heart does not will to repent or believe. The human will is in bondage to lust. It is not free to turn to Christ. It must be made free. Ps. 110: 3. The conscience too is warped. Tit. 1: 15. But especially is the understanding of man depraved. He is in no position to sit in judgment upon the Scriptures. He needs to humble himself before the God of the Bible.

This concept of man's understanding being depraved

---

1. See bibliography for documentary information. All the extermination camps were situated in Poland as follows: Auschwitz-Birkenau (2,000,000 victims), Maidenek (1,380,000), Chelmo (600,000), Belzec (600,000), Treblinka (731,800) and Stutthof (67,500).

was, and is, ridiculed by the Higher Critics. According to them man is advancing and getting better all the time. Man is inherently upright and basically good. If there are defects, these are due to remnants of the ape still left after man's ascent up the evolutionary scale.

The mass exterminations of the Nazi régime have smashed this delusion that man is basically good. Systematically 12 million people, Gentiles and Jews, were murdered in cold blood by firing squads or in gas chambers. The German nation, the cradle of the Higher Critical Movement, was responsible.[1] There were hundreds of centres where massacres were organized. It took 7,000 Germans to operate the Auschwitz concentration camp alone.

The Bible declares, 'the heart of man is deceitful above all things and desperately wicked, who can know it?' Jer. 17: 9. Who can plumb and understand the seeds of tyranny and wickedness that lie ready to germinate in the heart of every unregenerate soul? Do you think this an exaggeration? Then read the following eye-witness account of an extermination by an S.S. officer who hanged himself in 1945.

'Next morning, just before seven, I was informed that the first transport was due to arrive in ten minutes. And, in fact, in a few minutes, the first train from Lemberg arrived. The 45 carriages contained 6,700 people; 1,450 of them were already dead on arrival.' But it is impossible to continue the quotation in which a detailed account is given of the death of all these people, even in abridged form. The whole thing is so monstrous and inhuman, so

---

1. *Out of the Night* by Michael Horbach. 1967. Vallentine Mitchel. 261 pp. £1.25. This extraordinary volume gives eye-witness accounts of Jews who miraculously survived extermination. Rare cases of outstanding courage by Germans who protected Jews are described.

sickening and repugnant that it would disgust and distress many. Those with a tough emotional constitution can find the material easily enough.[1] But the question must be faced: how do those who deny the Biblical doctrine of sin explain these barbarous atrocities?

2. The truth about the person of the Devil

The doctrine of Lucifer and the fallen angels is rejected and derided today. That Satan and a host of evil spirits have spiritual power to tempt, deceive, and corrupt men and women is regarded as a figment of the imagination, a surviving superstition of antiquity. The Bible is unswerving and uncompromising in its declaration that Satan and innumerable evil spirits of seductive genius conspire to fill men's hearts to do evil. Eph. 6: 12.

How else can one explain the diabolical genius and power wielded by Hitler and his grizzly monsters; Himmler, Goebbels, Kaltenbrunner, Jodl, Eichmann and the rest? A poor student, an undistinguished soldier, an unsuccessful house-painter who appalled statesmen by his ignorance and vulgarity – how could such a commonplace man mesmerize a whole nation and defy the world until countless millions lay slaughtered in the world's biggest massacre? How indeed, except by the power of the Devil who filled his heart and controlled his mind? One of his generals describes the beloved Fuehrer in one of his tantrums as follows: 'his fists raised, his cheeks flushed with rage, his whole body trembling, the man stood there in front of me – he was almost screaming, his eyes seemed to pop out of his head and the veins stood out in his temples.'[2] This performance is reputed to have lasted two hours.

---

1. ibid., p. 85.
2. *The Rise and Fall of the Third Reich*, W. L. Shirer, p. 1310.

Are we to believe that Hitler was alone in inspiring the misery and slaughter of millions of the human race? Can we not discern the sinister activity of the evil one at work in controlling the mind of this man who in terms of natural ability was very ordinary. The genius behind Hitler's ability to rouse the crowds and to retain leadership until Europe lay in ruins was more than human. It was Satanic.

3. The truth about reprobation

Why does God permit these calamities? The reason is plainly stated in the first chapter of Romans. 'And even as they did not like to retain God in their knowledge, God gave them over to a reprobate mind, to do those things which are not convenient; Being filled with all unrighteousness, fornication, wickedness, covetousness, maliciousness; full of envy, *murder*.' Rom. 1: 28.

It is impossible to be neutral in respect to God and his son Jesus Christ. 'He that is not for me, is against me,' said Jesus. Respectable neutrality is out of the question. Either we accept the truth that Jesus Christ is the only way of salvation or we reject it. 'I am the way, and the truth and the life' he said, 'no man cometh to the Father, but by me.' John 14: 6.

Before the holocaust of Europe, the masses had politely rejected the Gospel. Many people felt they did not need God, nor his Christ, nor his Bible. They did not like to retain God in their knowledge. They rejected Christ the Messiah. Both Jews and Gentiles rejected the doctrine of sin and salvation by the Lamb that was slain. They had no need of a sinbearer. They ridiculed the idea of Satan. They were respectable, self-righteous, decent people. Gospellers were just a nuisance. The people wanted God to leave them alone. And God did leave them alone. He left them to their own devices. The results are well known and what happened then is happening all over again under Communism.[1] History is repeating itself. Before the war it was the menace of Fascism. Now it is Communism. It seems that man will never learn that left to himself he is lost – physically, spiritually and eternally lost.

4. The truth about the Gospel

But God has not left us entirely. In those gas chambers there were Hebrew Christians who died trusting only in the sacrifice of Christ for the forgiveness of their sins.[2] Conversion meant nothing to the Nazis. All those with Jewish blood perished. Hebrew Christians perished too in the gas chambers. All over Europe there were those who, in the name of Christ, were prepared to die for their convictions rather than heed the dictates of the Nazi overlords. In addition to this, many turned to the Gospel through the suffering of the war, suffering which causes us to ask why is there sin, brutality and murder? These things cannot take place without leaving a fearful mark upon the conscience. And how can this guilt be removed? In answer to this question we discover the wonderful love of Christ. No matter how scarlet we are in vice he invites us to come to him. 'Come to me' he says, 'all ye that are

---

1. Latest documentation of torture, murder and persecution behind the Iron Curtain can be found in *Tortured for Christ* by Richard Wurmbrand (a Hebrew Christian), Hodder and Stoughton, and *In God's Underground* by the same author. Allen and Unwin.

2. The following quotation is from a letter received from The Barbican Mission to the Jews. 'With regard to the matter you raise about the question of Hebrew churches in Poland, up to 1939 our Society had several such churches in Balystock, Vilna and Warsaw. Most of the congregations and the pastors and their families did not survive the Nazi occupation. This should certainly prove to you that a large number of Hebrew Christians were involved in the Nazi extermination. The matter is too recent and painful for those who survived for there to be any personal details added.'

weary and heavy-laden, and I will give you rest.' To all those who turn to him, Christ grants forgiveness of sin and eternal life. If a man repents and truly believes in Christ, he shall be saved even if guilty of the most shameful acts. The dying thief turned, believed, and lived, in his last hour upon earth.

God is not dead! Cruel and wicked men are being transformed all over the world – Vietnam, New Guinea, Peru. I have seen this happen recently in my own pastorate. God continues to give new hearts to the godless – to respectable sinners and to open transgressors. He can give a new heart to Rubinstein. He gives new life to Communist torturers. God is alive. Christ is calling. He invites us to come to him as we are; *today*.

Two main points have emerged so far. Firstly, the promise that 'all Israel shall be saved' stands firm and unalterable. What God declares, that he will perform. Is anything too hard for him? Secondly, we observe that Jewry has survived. The attempt to destroy the Hebrew race was directed at their strongest point: Europe, particularly Poland, the most religious and virile centre of Jewry. Almost three million Polish Jews perished. The way of the diaspora back to the land of their fathers had begun in concept way back in 1862[1] followed by four waves of immigration.[2] World War II resulting in helpless plight for innumerable Jewish refugees brought about the fifth wave and contributed greatly towards Israel becoming a separate nation in 1948. One of the results of the attempted extermination, therefore, was the consolidation of the new Jewish state which has served as never before since the time of Christ to focus attention on the Jews – who they are – their beliefs – their place in the world.

Now in conclusion we need to stand back and view the general position of Jews in the world today and face up to the question of their evangelization. The promise is that

---

1. The revival of Zionism with the idea of a 'return to Zion' can be traced in the publication of books from 1862 onwards.
2. In the first wave, 1880–1900, came the tillers of the soil. In the second, 1900–1914, came the scientific farmers to build up the country's agriculture. Speculators, industrialists and educationalists arrived with the third, 1918–24, and intellectuals, professionals and bureaucrats in the fourth, 1924–39. In broad terms this describes the *aliyah* or immigration wave.

the Hebrew people as a body will be converted. Whether this means the Jews of Israel or large numbers of Jews throughout the diaspora we cannot tell. It may mean Israel only; it may mean both; it is unlikely that the dispersed Jews alone are meant because of territorial implications already discussed. In surveying the position it will be helpful to view the state of the diaspora first and then of Israel the nation.

The Diaspora

The United States and Russia, the two foremost nations of the world, contain the largest number of Jews. There are an estimated five and a half million in the U.S.A.,[1] 75 per cent of which lives in the large cities. (Over two million in New York, 500,000 in Los Angeles, 330,000 in Philadelphia and 185,000 in Boston.) According to official statistics given in 1963 there are 2,267,814 citizens registered as Jews in the Soviet Union. But as author Ben Ami shows, many Jews have hidden their identity so that the estimate of three and a half million is valid.

One cannot help observing that the more prosperous countries contain large numbers of Jews.[2] There are

---

1. Judaism like Christianity is divided into denominations. *Reform Judaism* had its roots in Germany in the early part of the nineteenth century. A movement known as *Conservative Judaism* broke away from *Reform Judaism* and gained in proportions. Now these two groups along with *Orthodox Judaism* form the main Jewish denominations in the U.S.A. with congregations in Europe and Africa. Outside the U.S.A. orthodoxy is almost uncontested as the main denomination. Small dissenting bodies exist such as *Reconstruction* and *Jewish Science*.
2. Historians have commented upon the fact that Spain, once a foremost nation, has never been the same since the Inquisition which led to the expulsion of a large Jewish population in 1492. There are only about 5,000 Jews in Spain today. Portugal ejected her Jewish community in 1496.

530,000 in France, 410,000 in Britain,[1] 280,000 in Canada, 114,000 in South Africa and 475,000 in the Argentine. Before Hitler's rise to power, in 1933, a census showed that there were about 500,000 Jews in Germany. By the outbreak of war this number had dropped by emigration to 215,000, of which number about 25,000 survived the Nazi purge by one means or another.

A full discussion of the principles which underlie the propagation of the Gospel among these Jews dispersed throughout the free world lies outside the scope of this study. Reference can only be made to major points.

It has been widely acknowledged that local churches which are spiritually healthy provide the best basis for Jewish evangelism. Special faith missions have sold the idea that only specially trained workers (preferably Hebrew Christians) can successfully meet the task of Jewish evangelization. But experience has proved that Jews come to a knowledge of salvation in the same way and by the same means as Gentiles. Conviction of sin through the moral law, the creation of a spiritual appetite, a desire for assurance, friendly relationships with Christians: these are the means invariably used in their salvation.

That special equipment and study is desirable for those working permanently among the Jews is not disputed. A Gentile, George Bowes, of the London City Mission, devotes his life both to working among Jews and attempting to co-ordinate the efforts of some eight or nine separate special missions to Jews with headquarters in London. He declares that it took him about two years really to grasp the Jewish way of thought. Interviews with him and other workers among Jews, particularly Hebrew Christians,

---

1. This figure is based upon an article in the *Jewish Chronicle* 19 April 1968, which indicated that Anglo-Jewry is in a state of numerical decline.

confirmed that the same basic principles apply to the evangelization of Jews as to any other group. Determination, love and perseverance must join hands with sound theology and a knowledge of the human mind. A profound knowledge of Judaism and Jewish history is helpful but by no means essential.

The great majority of Jews today possess little religious knowledge and are governed by the same basic unspiritual and materialistic notions as Gentiles. Ungodliness is their chief characteristic as is the case with the Gentiles. If they are to be saved it will be through the entrance of *The Word* which gives light. All the basic themes of the Gospel: the attributes of God, sin, atonement, regeneration and providence, apply with the same force to Jews as to Gentiles. Technical arguments about the interpretation of the Messianic passages are in most cases far less profitable, as a starting point, than a straightforward study of the nature of sin and need of atonement. Jesus wasted no time in directing the mind of the rich young ruler to the moral law and highlighted his covetousness in loving his worldly possessions more than God. Our Lord did not involve himself with technical arguments when he met the intensely religious Nicodemus. He simply asserted the necessity of the new birth and chided Nicodemus for his ignorance of that fundamental matter. John 3.

We owe much to special Jewish missions both for their prolonged service among Jews and for their work in reminding churches of the priority of the Jews in respect of the Gospel. Nevertheless it must be remembered that societies or special organizations can never replace the local churches in evangelization. The latter form God's supreme agent for evangelizing the world.[1] Organizations

---

1. This is expounded in *God-Centred Evangelism* by R. B. Kuiper. Banner of Truth.

and missions, much more than churches, are prone to spiritual disease. There is the chronic concern for 'the mission', competition with other missions, internal squabbles, the problem of authority and the time-consuming search for openings among the churches. Missions lack the oversight of scripturally appointed elderships and often there is a clash of loyalty between the mission and the church. Seldom do special missions constitute a balanced happy family of all kinds and conditions of men, which is a mark of a vigorous local church. Moreover, a spiritually strong church provides an ideal base for an expository teaching ministry. These questions should be asked, firstly: would not some of the talented members of Jewish missions be better employed as permanent *church-based* workers? And secondly: are churches bordering on or situated in large Jewish communities ready to assimilate and support such workers? These are important questions as we consider the evangelization of Jews in Western countries. Whether in Golders Green or Hove, the Jews keep together. Wherever they are found, the responsibility for their evangelism must always belong to the local church. This being so, we must admit that reformation and revival among the churches are prime requisites if the Jews of the diaspora are to find salvation in their Messiah.

Israel

In England today about nine out of ten people have slender contact with the Established Church through christening, marriage and burial. In other words they are only nominally Christian. A similar position pertains in Israel where most Israelis do not attend synagogues. Circumcision is carried out, not by a local Rabbi, but by a Mohel or Circumciser. Marriage and burial services are mostly cared for by State departments.

Religious fervour varies greatly in intensity. In some quarters the Sabbath is rigidly observed. Religious zeal is often confused with national patriotism.

It is difficult to see where the impetus would come from for Israel's conversion to Christianity. It seems a sheer impossibility. One could seek for signs of hope from the surrounding nations or from Christian groups within Israel, but a survey of the Christian churches in the Middle East reveals a state of pathetic weakness. It has not always been so. The German historian Adolf von Harnack estimated that 90 per cent of Asia Minor was at least nominally converted to Christianity by the year A.D. 100 as the direct result of the missionary work of the apostles, particularly Paul. Today a Moslem monopoly surrounds Israel. Evangelical churches are puny in size and feeble in strength. Nowhere in the world has there been less encouragement to missionaries than in the Arab countries, and we look in vain for impetus from them for the evangelization of Israel.

What about the Christian community within Israel? The 60,000 Christians are split into Greek Catholics, Greek Orthodox, Roman Catholics, Maronites, and a number of widely diversant Protestant groups which represent a fragmented approach. Evangelicals are few and far between and those of robust Reformed convictions rarer still. Missionaries find that prejudice against Christianity on account of past persecutions is formidable and discouraging. Moreover, it is difficult to divorce Hitler's extermination from the minds and hearts of the Israelis. Normal channels of gaining a foothold by teaching Christianity in schools is difficult since Judaism is solidly entrenched. Prospects of a Christian revival in Israel are very bleak indeed.

What of the possibility of a Christian revival springing from the synagogues of Israel? There is no doubt that there is a search for fresh meaning in the country. To use the words of Julius Gould writing in *New Society*,[1] 'The State of Israel has provided a focus in a way which reaches far more Jews than the Jewish religion itself.' He declares that Israelis 'aim to provide a moral example, a social example – to spread a message from Israel to the world', yet he admits that the message is as yet undefined. It is unrealistic therefore to hope that truth will suddenly leap out of darkness.

Present-day conditions would suggest that the conversion of the Jews to the Gospel is impossible. But the territorial restoration of Israel is in itself a token of encouragement. Spurgeon, preaching in 1864 on the Restoration of the Jews from the passage in Ezekiel on the Dry Bones declared: 'Israel is now blotted out from the map of nations; her sons are scattered far and wide; her daughters mourn beside all the rivers of the earth. Her sacred song is hushed; no king reigns in Jerusalem; she bringeth forth no governors among her tribes. But she is to be restored; she is to be restored "as from the dead". When her own sons have given up all hope of her, then is God to appear for her. She is to be re-organized; her scattered bones are to be brought together. There will be a native government again; there will again be the form of a body politic; a state shall be incorporated, and a king shall reign. Israel has now become alienated from her own land. Her sons, though they can never forget the sacred dust of Palestine, yet die at a hopeless distance from her consecrated shores. But it shall not be so for ever, for her sons shall again rejoice in her; her land shall be called Beulah, for as a young man marrieth a virgin so shall her sons marry her. 'I will place you in your own land,' is God's promise to them.

---

1. 29 June 1967.

Have not these words been fulfilled in an astonishing way?

Concerning the spiritual conversion of the Jews, Spurgeon went on to say: 'Looking at this matter, we are very apt to say, "How can these things be? How can the Jews be converted to Christ? How can they be made into a nation? Truly, the case is quite as hopeless as that of the bones in the valley! How shall they cease from worldliness, or renounce their constant pursuit of riches? How shall they be weaned from their bigoted attachment to their Talmudic traditions? How shall they be lifted up out of that hardness of heart, which makes them hate the Messiah of Nazareth, their Lord and King? How can these things be?" The prophet does not say it cannot be; his unbelief is not so great as that, but at the same time, he scarcely ventures to think that it can ever be possible. He very wisely, however, puts back the question upon his God – "O Lord God, thou knowest." Now some of you are very sanguine about this tonight, and you are expecting to see the Jews converted very soon, perhaps in a month or two. I wish you may see it as soon as your desires would date it. Others of us are not very sanguine, but take a more gloomy view of a long future of woes. Well, let us both together come before God tonight, and say "O Lord God, thou knowest; and if thou knowest it, Lord, we will be content to leave the secret with thee; only tell us what thou wouldst have us to do; we ask not food for speculation, but we do ask for work; we ask for something by which we may practically show that we really do love the Jew, and that we would bring him to Christ." In answer to this, the Lord says to his servants, "*Prophesy upon these bones*," so that our duty tonight, as Christians, is to prophesy upon these bones, and we shall then see God's purpose fulfilled, when we obey God's precept.'

This exhortation from just over a century ago is relevant

today. Let the emphasis be placed on prayer united with endeavour. Let us not think anything too hard for God. What is impossible with men is possible with him. Why should God's best belong to yesterday? Can we say that Jesus has lost the dew of his youth? The greater the enemy the greater the victory. What formidable obstacles impeded the 'ignorant and unlearned' fishermen of Pentecost. Yet they turned the world upside down. What darkness prevailed in 1500 A.D. How different the scene in 1600 A.D.! How few believers in 1800: how huge the increase by 1971! The apostles of despair would have us believe the position to be beyond recovery and with one third the world under Communism there is cause enough for gloom.

But what of emerging nations? – nations large and small, just born into the modern world? Can we say with certainty that God has no purpose, no revivals, no mercy for the millions of Brazil, Nigeria, Indonesia, New Guinea, Nepal, the Transkei, Sabah or Equador?

In contrast to the spiritual invalids of our day who bemoan 'that the former days were better than these,' Ecc. 7: 10, Paul, filled with the spirit of prophecy, gazed into the future, and saw harvests of souls, the fruits of Calvary, gathering upon gathering – amazed at the vastness and wisdom of it all he cried out, 'O the depth of the riches both of the wisdom and knowledge of God! how unsearchable *are* his judgments, and his ways past finding out! For who hath known the mind of the Lord? or who hath been his counsellor? Or who hath first given to him, and it shall be recompensed unto him again? For of him, and through him, and to him, *are* all things: to whom be glory for ever. Amen.'

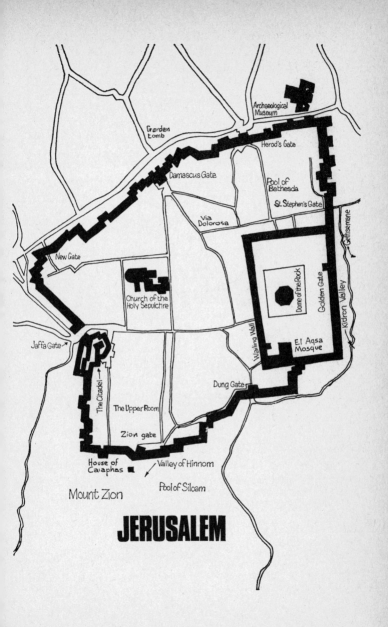

Garden
Tomb

Archaeological
Museum

Herod's Gate

Damascus Gate

Pool of
Bethesda

St Stephen's Gate

Via
Dolorosa

New Gate

Gethsemane

Church of the
Holy Sepulchre

Dome of the Rock

Golden Gate

Kidron Valley

Jaffa Gate

Wailing Wall

El Aqsa
Mosque

The Citadel

Dung Gate

The Upper Room

Zion gate

House of
Caiaphas

Valley of Hinnom

Pool of Siloam

Mount Zion

JERUSALEM

JERUSALEM

*'Thus saith the Lord God; This is Jerusalem:
I have set it in the midst of the nations
and countries that are round about her.'* Ezekiel 5: 5.

Jerusalem from her birth to the present day has her own
story, a tale quite different from that of other cities.
Flanked by the barren waste of Sinai on the south, mountains to the east and sea to the west, the City of God is
insulated from the nations. Paradoxically this insularity
is combined with centrality, for Jerusalem is the compass
point to three continents whose trade routes have passed
her gates. The road from the Nile Valley to the massive
civilizations and cultures around the Euphrates has clung
close to Jerusalem. Here, in a city at once central and
separate, it has pleased God to display the true religion.
Jerusalem is a city set upon a hill which cannot be hid.
Other cities have become famous because they occupy a
central position in some vast industrial complex or because
they lie on a river estuary. Jerusalem is a rocky outcrop
removed from sea, estuary and industry.

Old Jerusalem was once much more of a fortress than
it is now. Over the centuries the deep ravines surrounding
the rocky plateau have filled up by more than sixty feet.
This volume of debris is an epic, written in geographical
terms, of plunder and destruction. In both Hebrew and
Arabic the word 'Salem' – 'Shalom' means 'peace' –
Jerusalem: city of peace. Ironically, no place has been
more the subject of dispute or war than this city. Fought
over for 3,000 years this stone plateau is more than ever
the centre of world debate, for Jerusalem is at the same
time City of David, City of Christ and City of Mohammed.
The three monotheistic religions contest this centre. All

three find their genesis in Abraham: the Arabs descend from Ishmael, the Jews from Isaac, and Christians claim that by their new birth they are the spiritual progeny of their father Abraham. Rom. 4: 11. Gal. 3: 7. Setting aside the claims of Mohammed, it can be said that Jerusalem has borne witness to the truth of God – first through Judaism, and from the time of Pentecost to all peoples and nations of the earth. '*This is Jerusalem: I have set it in the midst of the nations.*' Ez. 5: 5.

Early Scenes

Whether or not Melchisedek, King of Salem, made this actual spot his home is disputed. We may with more certainty believe that Mount Moriah – the Holy Mountain witnessed the sacrifice of Isaac by Abraham. If the blood of Isaac, in the final outcome, did not join itself with the earth of that place, the blood of the ram, symbol of substitution, did. So did blood far more precious than that of a ram. Mount Moriah was the place destined to cast its shadows over the agony by crucifixion of God's Son. 'Behold,' cried John the Baptist, 'the *Lamb of God*, which taketh away the sin of the world.' No event, apart from the resurrection, is more important to Christians than the Cross of Golgotha – place of the skull – a part of Mount Moriah. The momentous transaction, by means of which believers receive God's righteousness for their justification, and in which 'the iniquities of us all' were laid on the sinless Son of God must be in view to the concourse of nations. '*Thus said the Lord God: This is Jerusalem: I have set it in the midst of the nations.*' Jerusalem, where prophets of old were martyred, had to be the place where the Prophet of Prophets would suffer for the sins of the people.

Isaac, Abraham's only begotten son, typified God's only begotten Son. Abraham received God's approbation for his obedience. 'By myself have I sworn, saith the Lord, for because thou has done this thing, and hast not withheld thy son, thine only son: that in blessing I will bless thee, and in multiplying I will multiply thy seed as the stars of the heaven, and as the sand which is upon the sea shore; and thy seed shall possess the gate of his enemies; And in thy seed shall all the nations of the earth be blessed.' Gen. 22: 16–18.

Heaven and earth will sooner pass away than God fail in his promise, so that in the course of time Abraham's seed multiplied exceedingly. With a mighty hand the new nation was brought out of Egypt's bondage by Moses and purified in the wilderness of Sinai. Then under Joshua it made conquest of the enemies' gates in Canaan; to possess the hills and valleys promised to them by an unbreakable covenant. In due time David seized the city of the Jebusites for his own, Joab, his captain, ascending a water duct cut in solid rock to throw open the gates to the invaders. The holy mount became David's capital and before long the 'Ark of the Covenant', the symbol of God's presence with His people, was brought to Jerusalem. The time had come to build a temple to house the Ark. This privilege was denied to David, since he was a man of blood. It fell to his son, King Solomon, the wisest of men, to achieve the temple dream. The work was incredible in its beauty. Only a man of Solomon's genius could have completed so great a wonder of architectural magnificence in the short time of seven years. It was dedicated in 960 B.C. As beautiful as the temple itself were the prayers of King Solomon on that memorable day of ceremony. He prayed that, if the Jews were taken away into captivity because of their sin, they might be forgiven 'if they return to thee with all their heart and pray toward the city which thou hast chosen, and toward the house which I have built for thy name.' II Chron. 6: 38.

The Jewish people reached the apex of their military prowess under David: their widest geographical extension under Solomon. But subsequently division and decline begin to eat away the strength of the nation. Retrogression was rapid among the ten tribes that broke away under Jeroboam I to form the Northern Kingdom. The mysterious disappearance of the ten tribes dates from the time of their dispersion in 722 B.C. after the Assyrians had made conquest of the land under Tiglath-Pileser and Shalmaneser. However, when King Sennacherib attempted to conquer the Southern Kingdom of Judah, God intervened with a stroke of crippling devastation. For presuming to reproach Jehovah and for trampling in pride upon that which was holy, a hundred-and-eighty-five thousand of his troops were swept away in one night. Is. 37: 36.

Destruction and Captivity

The destruction of Jerusalem was postponed. Jeremiah followed Isaiah, confirming the latter's threats that the end was near. Jeremiah couched his warnings in desperate terms. It was of no avail. 586 B.C. proved to be the fateful year of downfall. King Nebuchadnezzar of Babylon came upon Jerusalem; the magnificent temple was reduced to rubble and the city mutilated and torn. Jerusalem's best sons were carried away captive, to compose songs of lamentation by the banks of Euphrates.

The Hebrew people have always been divided – the lovers of mammon on the one hand: devout servants of Jehovah on the other. When under the prophet Nehemiah and the priest Ezra a new day of opportunity dawned to rebuild the temple and repair the walls of the Holy City, only a minority chose to leave their hard-earned prosperity and night-life of Babylon.

The journey home was arduous. Peril stalked the

pilgrims, some 43,000 in number. Yet they won their way back. With the help of fervent exhortations from Haggai the prophet, the sanctuary was re-erected. Some of the aged veteran Jews wept when the foundations of the second temple were dedicated. Ezra 3: 12. They remembered the former glory. This was brass compared with the golden splendour of Solomon's sanctuary. Haggai comforted the people, describing the inferior structure in the following terms: 'The glory of this latter house shall be greater than of the former, saith the Lord of hosts.' Hag. 2: 9. These words were to find their fulfilment in the advent of the Lord of hosts himself, who, to use the words of Malachi, would 'suddenly come to his temple'. Mal. 3: 1.

Before the Messiah's coming the sanctuary was subject to desecrations which maddened the Jews. First came the Greeks who, under the leadership of the much-hated Antiochus Epiphanes IV, erected a gigantic statue of Jupiter Olympus behind the altar of sacrifice in 167 B.C. Within the sacred courts the melody of Hebrew psalmody was silenced by lewd revels and ugly scenes of profligacy. Anguish prostrated the Hebrew people. Their indignation was soon to lead to open rebellion. The flames of guerrilla warfare constantly burned the feet of their Hellenist overlords. This conflict became known as the Maccabean war, so called after the Jewish leader, Mattathias Maccabaeus (The Hammer) who had five sons: John, Simon, Judas, Eleazar and Jonathan. Between them they possessed brilliant gifts of leadership. Judas in particular was a tactician, brimful of military artfulness, and his genius continually confounded the enemy. Although equipped with primitive weapons and handicapped by an army of inferior size, Judas eventually swept into Jerusalem, cleared the temple of its debris, destroyed the hated altar of Zeus, purified the sanctuary and relit the lamps of the *menorah* (seven-branched candlestick). To this day, while Christians celebrate their Christmas, the Jews commemorate 'Hanukkah' – the Feast of Lights – an eight-day festival beginning on 25 December.

The Maccabean era lasted for a century until in 62 B.C. Pompey, his sword dripping with blood, rode triumphantly into Jerusalem. The Holy City was but one more prize added to the long list of Roman conquests.

From now on Judean sovereignty was no more. The people were taxed ruthlessly. Now appeared the detested publican (the tax collector). In 37 B.C. Herod, the son of Antipater, an Idumean (Edomite), and puppet to the Roman hierarchy, was placed upon the throne of government. The Jews loathed him. As cunning as he was proud, his imagination teemed with fantastic schemes for building. Most ambitious of all his ideas was the reconstruction of the temple, a work which began in 19 B.C., continued during the time of Christ's ministry and did not end until A.D. 64. This labour, massive in its proportions, was accomplished by an enormous army of workmen, combined with subtlety, for it was important not to give the Jews the impression that the old temple was really being replaced. Although only half-complete during the time of the ministry of our Lord, the temple was always in use. The veil hiding the Holy of Holies was kept secure. Behind it was an empty space. The ark, destroyed by Nebuchadnezzar, no longer existed.

The terraces were constructed with granite blocks up to sixty feet in length. In some places the walls were equivalent in height to a forty-five storey block of flats or offices today. Indeed the construction was fabulous and we can well understand why our Lord's disciples sought to elicit their master's comments upon this extraordinary blend of architectural ambition and engineering skill. We can also imagine their dismay when he declared that the seemingly immovable stones would, within one generation, be thrown down. How could this glorious temple be destroyed?

This was the city and temple over which Our Lord wept, 'Saying, If thou hadst known, even thou, at least in this thy day, the things which belong unto thy peace! but now they are hid from thine eyes. For the days shall come upon thee, that thine enemies shall cast a trench about thee, and compass thee round, and keep thee in on every side; and shall lay thee even with the ground, and thy children within thee; and they shall not leave in thee one stone upon another; because thou knewest not the time of thy visitation.' Luke 19: 42–44. This was the Jerusalem of which our Lord said, 'Jerusalem shall be trodden down of the Gentiles, until the times of the Gentiles be fulfilled.' Luke 21: 24.

It is evident from this latter prophecy that there is to be a termination in the course of time to Gentile domination over Jerusalem. These words also give warrant to careful observation of events concerning the Holy City. It is important therefore that we review the Jerusalem history up to the present time.

The A.D. Years

Seething hatred of Roman dominion erupted into open violence in A.D. 66. The Jews were aided once more by brilliant leadership, this time in the person of Simon bar-Giora. The Jerusalem garrison, taken by surprise, was vanquished by the rebels. The Emperor Nero dispatched Vespasian, his most competent general, with 60,000 men, to quell the uprising. Nero died in A.D. 68 and Vespasian, after a brief interval, hurried back to Rome, leaving Titus, his son, in command. A strategist of the first order, Titus proceeded to 'cast a trench round' the Holy City.

Famine soon seized the populace. Yet the Jews fought

back with savage determination. Gigantic siege machines were moved up to the walls. The Jews smashed them furiously. Soldiers attempting to scale the walls were subjected to boiling oil and huge stones hurled from above. Exasperation drove the Romans to fearful acts of barbarity. Jewish prisoners were crucified five hundred at a time. Others had their hands cut off. Starvation, disillusionment, division took the city by the throat and made it a living hell. Defeat was inevitable. The figure of 600,000 Jews dead through starvation, disease or battle, provided by the Roman historian Tacitus, is probably more reliable than that of a million given by Josephus, a Jew, regarded by his fellows as a traitor of the foulest kind.

Victory cost the Romans more than they bargained for. They retaliated by humiliating the Jews to the utmost degree. Destruction opened her jaws to devour not only the temple and the Holy City, but the Jewish State as well. The price of a Jew on the slave market fell in value to the equivalent of a horse.

Smarting under the agonies of defeat, the Jews refused to accept their fate. Three fortresses still held out and it was only in A.D. 73, that Masada, situated by the Dead Sea, was captured. The vast ramp built by the Romans at Masada is to be seen today: a grim memorial of that last siege. In centres of Jewish dispersion revolts against the Roman yoke broke out in A.D. 115 – in Egypt, Libya, Cyrenaica and Cyprus.

Another Simon, this time Simon bar-Kochba, as astute as his predecessor, headed a rebellion which began in 132. It lasted until A.D. 135. This led to the destruction of a further 580,000 Jews. To forestall more trouble the Romans dispersed the remaining Jews to the four corners of the Empire. 'All of Judaea became almost a desert' wrote Dio Cassius, a Roman author.

During the seventy years of upheaval from A.D. 66 to

A.D. 135 the disciples of Jesus separated themselves from Judaism, the parent religion. The Christian Church in its origin naturally saw Hebrew Christians numerically predominant, but as time wore on conversions from Jewry became very rare. As for Jerusalem, it was now thoroughly Gentile. On only one day a year were the Jews permitted entry.

During the seventh century the shadow of Islam fell across Mount Moriah. Caliph Omar arrived outside the walls in A.D. 638. The small Gentile population were in no position to resist. The take-over was peaceful as were the four centuries which followed. The Mosque known as the Dome of The Rock was built between A.D. 687 and 691. It stands today: an ominous barrier to Jewish ambitions to build a third temple on the sacred site.[1]

Crusaders took Jerusalem by storm in 1099. The carnality of these ill-motivated champions of secular Christianity makes a sickening story. Blood again deluged the streets of the city whose name is Peace. After engaging in shameful slaughter, these blind bigots conducted a weeping procession along the route that Jesus once trod to Calvary. Certainly this was Gentile, not Christian, domination. It lasted until the recapture of the city by the Mohammedans in 1187. For 700 years thereafter the crescent drank the sunshine of the Judean hills.

Napoleon took Jerusalem in 1798, but it was soon retrieved by the Turks. The city remained with them until almost the end of the First World War, when Britain became the custodian of Palestine, including Jerusalem. All Britain's efforts to reconcile Jews and Arabs failed,

---

1. Horatius Bonar gives fourteen reasons why the claim made by some that the Dome of the Rock was originally the Christian Church of San Sophia cannot be correct. See *Imperial Bible Dictionary*, edited by Patrick Fairbairn.

and in 1948, much to her relief, her Mandate for Palestine ended. The state of Israel was immediately proclaimed by Israeli leader David Ben-Gurion and nine months' warfare – the first of three Arab–Israeli wars – ensued. When hostilities ended the Jerusalem area was divided between Transjordan and Israel. The United Nations armistice Commission gave Old Jerusalem to Transjordan.

Against all the dictates of prudence, King Hussein of Jordan made one with President Nasser just prior to the Six-day war of June 1967. This spelt disaster for Jordan. After a brief spell of bitter fighting the Israelis captured the old city on 7 June. Generals Dayan, Rabin and Narkiss made their way to the Wailing Wall at 2.00 p.m. Following a Jewish tradition, General Dayan wrote out a prayer and slipped the note between the joints of the wall, witness to centuries of violence. The note read: 'let peace reign in Jerusalem.' Standing on that historic spot General Dayan declared, 'we have returned to our holiest of holy places, never to be parted from it again.'

These were the events reported in the newspapers of the world. The Jerusalem of our day is the Jerusalem which God has set in the midst of the nations. The Lord Jesus Christ implied that we should watch the fortunes of the city of peace. The termination of Gentile domination is the signal of a new epoch. What does the future hold for the Jews? Indeed what does the future hold for us and our children? The skies have long been black with clouds of judgment. What possibly can turn the Almighty Creator from visiting us with wrath for our sins? What, indeed, apart from his mercy, his covenant of grace, and his promise that salvation is not only to visit Israel but all the ends of the earth!

DIFFERENT PROPHETIC VIEWS OUTLINED[1]

In Chapter 32 of the *Westminster Confession of Faith* we find a statement which is typical of historic Christian belief as regards the main points of eschatology – the last things.

This chapter reads as follows:

'1. God hath appointed a day wherein he will judge the world in righteousness by Jesus Christ, to whom all power and judgment is given of the Father. In which day, not only the apostate angels shall be judged, but likewise all persons that have lived upon earth shall appear before the tribunal of Christ, to give an account of their thoughts, words, and deeds, and to receive according to what they have done in the body, whether good or evil.

'2. The end of God's appointing this day is for the manifestation of the glory of his mercy in the eternal salvation of the elect, and of his justice in the damnation of the reprobate, who are wicked and disobedient. For then shall the righteous go into everlasting life, and receive that fulness of joy and refreshing which shall come from the presence of the Lord; but the wicked, who know not God, and obey not the gospel of Jesus Christ, shall be cast into eternal torments, and be punished with everlasting destruction from the presence of the Lord, and from the glory of his power.

'3. As Christ would have us to be certainly persuaded that there shall be a day of judgment, both to deter all men from sin, and for the greater consolation of the godly in

---

1. This outline almost wholly based on that provided by G. I. Williamson in his valuable commentary on the *Westminster Confession of Faith* is included by his permission. Having edited it and made additions any criticism should be laid at my door.

their diversity; so will he have that day unknown to men, that they may shake off all carnal security, and be always watchful, because they know not at what hour the Lord will come; and may be ever prepared to say Come, Lord Jesus, come quickly. Amen.'

Briefly summarized this chapter from the confession teaches us:

1. That God has appointed a day of general judgment.
2. That Christ will be the judge.
3. That all angels and men will appear before him.
4. That they will be judged for every thought, word, and deed.
5. That God's purpose in appointing this day is the mani-festation of his glorious justice and grace.
6. That the righteous and wicked will then enter upon their eternal reward, and
7. That the great day cannot be predicted or known before it comes.

The main fact to bear in mind is that we are to believe that at the last day there will be a great resurrection of the dead both of the just and unjust and that immediately after the resurrection there will be the general and final judgment of angels and men. John 5: 28. Rev. 20: 12, 13.

Because of belief in a literal millennium, groups have arisen which divide the resurrection into phases. These groups are pre-millennial or dispensationalist in character and it will be helpful to set out systematically the various viewpoints. There are four main groups to consider:

1. POST-MILLENNIALISM.

Post-millennialism has unfortunately been misrepresented, particularly in America. Some have confused it with the purely naturalistic and modernistic teaching that the world is going to become a utopia.

A true post-millennialism is entirely consistent with the teaching of the Westminster Confession quoted above.

Most post-millennialists believe:

1. That the Holy Spirit will gradually bring about a period of virtual triumph of true Christianity before Christ returns.

2. Some believe that a great apostasy will precede the 'golden age', others (perhaps most) believe that it will follow it. (Some believe that the Papacy at its height was the great apostasy, and that the Reformation began the course of events that will bring about the golden age.)

3. Christ will return after the world is evangelized, the Jews converted (en masse) and the Church established in great purity and unity.

4. The resurrection will be general (all men at the same time).

5. The general judgment will follow.

6. Then the eternal kingdom will begin.

Post-millennialists believe that the Kingdom of God is a present reality, that it is spiritual in character, and that the Church is the divine institution which effects this coming of Christ in his kingdom power. John 18: 36, Luke 17: 20, Matt. 16: 19, Col. 1: 13, Dan. 2: 44, etc. They point to such passages as the following to prove that Christ's kingdom is in existence, and that it is a fulfilment of Old Testament prophecies. Acts 15: 14–18, Heb. 12: 22, 23, etc. Cf. Acts 2: 34–36, Psalm 110: 1, Eph. 1: 20, Col. 3: 1, Heb. 1: 3, 13, 8; 1.

2. A-MILLENNIALISM.

A-millennialists do not believe that the Bible predicts a golden age in world history prior to Christ's return nor do they believe that it predicts such an age in history after Christ's return before the final judgment. They believe:

1. That there will be a progressive maturation of the forces of good and evil. Matt. 13: 24–30, 37–43, 47–50.

2. Some believe there will be a tribulation and much (or great) apostasy throughout this era, while others believe

that the apostasy, II Thess. 2, will come as an event
concentrated in time immediately prior to Christ's
return.

3. Some believe that there will be no sign of Christ's return,
   while a few believe there will be –
   (a) the great (concentrated in time) apostasy.
   (b) conversion of the Jews.
   (c) a state of affairs in which it can be said that the
       gospel has been preached to all nations.

4. Christ will return and resurrect all men at the same time.

5. The general judgment will follow.

6. The new heaven and new earth will appear to abide for
   ever.

A-millennialists have become one of the strongest prophetic
groups in England and tend to predominate among the Reformed. Most Post-millennialists in England seem to have
originally adhered to A-millennialism.

In the United States of America the Lutherans form a strong
A-millennial group numbering about two million. Their confession of faith takes a militant A-millennial position as will
be seen from the following quotations:

'*Of the Millennium:*

With the Augsburg Confession, Art. XVII, we reject
every type of Millennialism, or Chiliasm, the opinions that
Christ will return visibly to this earth a thousand years
before the end of the world and establish a dominion of the
Church over the world; or that before the end of the world
the Church is to enjoy a season of special prosperity; or
that before the general resurrection on Judgment Day a
number of departed Christians or martyrs are to be raised
again to reign in glory in this world; or that before the end
of the world a universal conversion of the Jewish nation
(of Israel according to the flesh) will take place.

Over against this, Scripture clearly teaches, and we teach
accordingly, that the kingdom of Christ on earth will
remain under the cross until the end of the world, Acts 14:

22, John 16: 33; 18: 36, Luke 9: 23; 14: 27; 17: 20–37, II Tim. 4: 18, Heb. 12: 28, Luke 18: 8, that the second visible coming of the Lord will be His final advent, His coming to judge the quick and the dead, Matt. 24: 29, 30; 25: 31, II Tim. 4: 1, II Thess. 2: 8, Heb. 9: 26–28, that there will be but one resurrection of the dead, John 5: 28; 6: 39, 40, that the time of the Last Day is, and will remain, unknown, Matt. 24: 42; 25: 13, Mark 13: 32, 37, Acts 1: 7, which would not be the case if the Last Day were to come a thousand years after the beginning of a millennium; and that there will be no general conversion, a conversion en masse, of the Jewish nation, Rom. 11: 7, II Cor. 3: 14, Rom. 11: 25, I Thess. 2: 16.

According to these clear passages of Scripture we reject the whole of Millennialism, since it not only contradicts Scripture, but also engenders a false conception of the kingdom of Christ, turns the hope of Christians upon earthly goals, I Cor. 15: 19, Col. 3: 2, and leads them to look upon the Bible as an obscure book.

Of the Antichrist:

As to the Antichrist we teach that the prophecies of the Holy Scriptures concerning the Antichrist, II Thess. 2: 3–12, I John 2: 18, have been fulfilled in the Pope of Rome and his dominion. All the features of the Antichrist as drawn in these prophecies, including the most abominable and horrible ones, for example, that the Antichrist 'as God Sitteth in the temple of God', II Thess. 2: 4, that he anathematizes the very heart of the Gospel of Christ, that is, the doctrine of the forgiveness of sins by grace alone, for Christ's sake alone, through faith alone, without any merit or worthiness in man, Rom. 3: 20–28, Gal. 2: 16, that he recognizes only those as members of the Christian Church who bow to his authority; and that, like a deluge, he had inundated the whole Church with his anti-Christian doctrines till God revealed him through the Reformation – these very features are the outstanding characteristics of the Papacy. Cf. Smalcald Articles. Triglot, p. 515, p. 401, S 45; M., pp. 336, 258. Hence we subscribe to the statement of our Confessions that the Pope is 'the very Antichrist'. Smalcald Articles. S Triglot, p. 475, S 10; M., p. 308.

3. PRE-MILLENNIALISM.

This view was held in the ancient era by Irenaeus and others. The main outline is as follows:

1. World history is to extend 6,000 years, a thousand years for each of the days of creation, cf. 2 Pet. 3: 8 (of course not all accept this particular point).

2. Towards the end of this period (the sixth day, which began with Christ's first coming) suffering and persecution of believers will increase until climaxed in the rise of Antichrist, cf. I Thess. 2: 3–10, I John 2: 18.

3. At the height of Antichrist's power Christ will appear in heavenly glory to triumph over all his enemies, resurrecting the saints and establishing his Kingdom which will last a thousand years (the seventh day, Sabbath, or Millennium). During this period Jerusalem will be rebuilt, the earth will prosper, and there will be universal peace.

4. At the end of this period the wicked will be raised for the final judgment.

5. Finally, the new creation will appear, cf. II Pet. 3, Rev. 22.

This basic scheme has had advocates throughout Church history, although this must be called a distinctly 'minority' view. In the nineteenth century this view became much more popular, and was held (with some variation) by such able scholars as Bengel, Godet, Van Oosterzee, Moorehead, and others. Then towards the end of the century and throughout the present century to an even greater degree, there has come a new and radically different type of pre-millennial doctrine. To this we now turn.

4. DISPENSATIONALISM.

Modern Dispensational Premillennialism can only be called a recent innovation. It is rather the product of the dispensational system, of which it is a part, than of the ancient teaching of the Christian Church. The dispensational pre-millennial scheme is as follows:

1. There are seven dispensations: Innocency (creation to the fall), Conscience (the fall to the flood), Human Government (the flood to the tower of Babel), Promise (from the patriarchs to Moses), Law (Moses to Christ), Grace (Christ to the Millennium), and Kingdom (the millennial period).

2. The nation (or kingdom) of Israel occupies a special place in the divine economy. It was the provisional form of the Kingdom of God. Because of apostasy it was overthrown, but the prophets predicted its re-establishment. The Messiah came and offered to establish this kingdom. The Jews refused. Christ was therefore forced to delay the establishment of the kingdom. He temporarily withdrew (going into a far country, Matt. 21: 33), but will return to do what he was then kept from doing.

3. The Church is regarded as a mere parenthesis in the history of the kingdom. It has no connection with the kingdom and was unknown to the prophets. It is a sort of unexpected 'break' which resulted in the 'windfall' of the gospel of grace for the nations. Most dispensationalists do not look for very profound results in the preaching of the Gospel. The real hope is only in Christ's return. The work of surpassing greatness will then follow in the millennial period.

4. Christ's return is imminent. He may come at any time. There are no predicted events which must first be fulfilled.

5. Christ's second coming will consist of two separate events (comings) with seven intervening years between. The first will be his coming for his saints, cf. Matt. 24: 40, 41, I Th. 4: 17. The second will follow the seven-year period in which the gospel of the kingdom will again be preached (by believing Jews), widespread conversion effected (though not universal), Israel reconstituted (some, however, put this event later), and in the latter part of this period Antichrist revealed and God's wrath poured out upon the human race, II Thess. 2, Rev. 16: 1f., Matt. 24: 14–22. After this period Christ will come with his saints. The living nations will then be judged, the saints that died during the great tribulation raised up, Antichrist destroyed, and Satan bound, Rev. 20: 1, 2.

6. The Millennial Kingdom will then be established. It will be an earthly, visible kingdom in which the Jews only will be natural citizens; the Gentiles will only be adopted citizens. Christ will sit on a throne in Jerusalem. The temple will be rebuilt, and sacrifices made once more, Ezek. 40–48. Universal peace and prosperity will prevail, Isa. 11 : 8, etc. During this period the world will be converted, some say by the Gospel, but most say, by might and by power.

7. At the end of the millennium Satan will be loosed for a little season. Gog and Magog will rise against the Holy city, Rev. 20: 7, 8. But God will intervene with fire from heaven. Satan will be cast into the pit, and the dead that have not yet been raised (i.e. the wicked) will be raised to appear before the judgement seat of God.

8. Then will follow the eternal kingdom of heaven.

MISUSE OF PROPHECY

Because many Christians, especially those young in the faith are easily misled some reference ought to be made, by way of warning, to the misuse of prophecy.

Misuse of prophecy among Jewish missions

Without undue disparagement of special missions to the Jews, it would seem (from the reports of some journalists) that for many of them preaching on prophecy is the means used to fill their coffers. For instance William Krutza writing in *Eternity*[1] magazine reports as follows in an article 'Let's rethink our approach to the Jews': 'The Fellowship of Christian Testimonies to the Jews reports a membership of eighty-five different agencies with 280 missionaries. This is by no means the total number of agencies or missionaries working among the Jews. . . . The multiplicity of organizations is an indication of the fragmented approaches.' Krutza goes on to say that all the Jewish evangelization missions he contacted reported that they were *dispensational*, and that 'upon listening to various Jewish evangelism radio broadcasts, such as "The Hebrew Christian Hour" with A. V. Michelson (heard on almost seventy stations in the U.S. and Canada), one gets the impression that Jewish evangelism is a secondary consideration. The primary emphasis of these broadcasts seems to be the presentation of only one rigid interpretation of the Bible.'

Concerning the radio ministry Belden Menkus, a frequent contributor to *Eternity*, observes that 'almost without exception the radio ministry of Jewish missions are on stations with a heavy budget of evangelical broadcasts. Programme content strongly emphasizes prophetic truths. In both instances the

---

1. *Eternity*, August 1967.

programme repels contemporary Jews but will strongly attract the type of evangelicals who can be counted on for contributions to the missions.'[1]

Prophecy a source of division among the churches

While the subject of prophecy is important it should never divide Christians, since differences in prophetic outlook need not overthrow basic beliefs essential to the Gospel. Many churches, particularly in the U.S.A., have been subject to tragic and unnecessary schisms over details of interpretation as the following quotation will illustrate:

'Reverend David B. came to the Green Meadows Church in June 1952. He made many changes in the first five months and encouraged a forward-looking programme in all phases of church life. He requested the organist to look for a choir director, feeling that one person could not do both tasks. He requested the official board to change the church secretary. She was a member of the church. He asked the Christian education committee to review the work of the teachers in the adult education department, and particularly to interview Mr. J. who had been teaching the Berea Class for eleven years. Mr. J. resigned.

'One month later, Reverend B. discussed with Mr. J. the teaching of the senior high class. Mr. J. stated that he did not agree with the minister's views on the coming of Christ and the world tribulation of the last days. The pastor became angry as the discussion continued, and insisted that as a scholar and specialist in this field his views should take precedence. Mr. J. coolly replied that after eleven years he had learned a few things himself.

'By the end of the year, the organist, church secretary and Mr. J. were meeting regularly to exchange notes concerning the minister who "was slowly ruining their church". The minister heatedly demanded that the board go on record as supporting his views in eschatology. The board was divided on the grounds that this was not the heart of the problem.

1. ibid.

'The pastor next called a congregational meeting and requested a vote of confidence in his Biblical scholarship and teaching ministry. The hostility which came out during the meeting left the pastor stupefied. The next day he wrote a letter to the congregation, announcing his resignation and calling on all true supporters of the Biblical view of the pre-tribulation rapture and premillennial return of Christ to arise as a testimony to the glory of God. They would meet in the Community Hall and hold services there as a purified church. Thirty-five per cent of the congregation took out their member-ship and a new church was formed.

'Now, several years later, no one can adequately explain what the separation was about. Some persons claimed that Mr. J. confided the minister had to leave over "a moral issue", but would not elaborate. Apparently to most it was a doctrinal issue, but most of the members of both churches confided to friends that they weren't quite sure what the pre-tribulation rapture meant. At any rate, Mr. J. is teaching the Berea Class and Reverend B. is still pastor of the new Church, although it took in only 125 new members since it was formed.'[1]

It is pathetic that there should be division of this nature and it cannot be too strongly asserted that differences of interpreta-tion about things to come should never divide evangelicals. Charity must provide a mantle of freedom under which differences can be freely discussed.

The magazine The Plain Truth

Happily there is less confusion and division over the subject of prophecy in Britain than in the U.S.A., yet many believers are inadequately taught. Hence they too easily imbibe the prophetic errors of a magazine like *The Plain Truth*. The latter boasts a circulation of a million copies per issue. This well-produced, magnificently illustrated, free magazine is

---

1. *Neurotics in the Church*, by Robert James St. Clair. Fleming H. Revell Company. pp. 128–129.

edited by Herbert W. Armstrong (assisted by his son Garner Ted Armstrong) the world-wide broadcaster. It is strongly sectarian in flavour so that many have thought the editor to be a Seventh Day Adventist, a fact which he strongly repudiates.[1]

This monthly has specialized in prophetic forecasts, especially on the Common Market, and made a feast of the Israeli issue. Like most sectarian bodies including the Mormons, Christadelphians and Jehovah Witnesses it is strongly literalist or chiliast in interpretation. Recent events in Israel according to *The Plain Truth* point to the imminent personal rule of Jesus Christ in Jerusalem. This will transpire after terrifying, imagination-defying, world-shaking tribulations have taken place, sometimes depicted in the magazine by lurid, ghastly drawings which must grip simple people and fill them with ardent desires to escape these woes. With their own new office and residential property in Jerusalem, *The Plain Truth* are all set to cover the event of the personal return of Christ.

Single texts ripped out of context and constant claims that *The Plain Truth* predictions have been fulfilled to the letter, characterize the magazine. Note the following claim together with the typically sectarian presentation: '*Germany* – believe it or not – *will* eventually be in Palestine, patrolling, policing – or on some other political excuse – occupying Jewish soil. Ezekiel 23, your own Bible, proves it. For further information write for our amazing free booklet, *1975 in Prophecy*. – Germany's eventual presence in Palestine will lead to a final *nuclear holocaust* – WORLD WAR III.'[2]

If a prediction such as this is fulfilled a feast will be made of the matter in subsequent issues (among survivors). Should the prediction fail it will be forgotten in the sands of time, there being little likelihood of anyone taking the matter up.

It is unfortunate that many have been deterred from a

---

1. *The Autobiography of Herbert W. Armstrong*. See p. 338.
2. *The Plain Truth*, July 1967. The quotation has been reproduced exactly, The italics are not mine.

study of prophecy, being repelled by the crude way in which the matter has been handled by many. The abuse of something good should not be permitted to blind us as to its value. Rich are the rewards for those who are patient, discreet and persevering in their study of this important subject.

APPENDIX C.

SELECT BIBLIOGRAPHY WITH COMMENTS

There is a danger of which I am well aware in classification of the kind which follows. A Biblical view of the future can hardly be circumscribed by details of the 'millennium' which, in any case, is taken by many to be a symbolical length of time. Personally I dislike being labelled 'post-millennial' and my conjecture is that most of those so 'classified' would not be altogether happy with the limitations inherent in such categories. Nevertheless for the sake of analysis and study classification cannot be avoided.

If I had to choose a name for the sake of conveying what I personally believe it would be rather a mouthful – a *royal redemptionist* – something of that nature, or an *optimistic soteriologist*! In other words I simply believe that Jesus reigns as king and that he has an invincible purpose to redeem a great many from the nations of the earth.

The universal Kingship of Christ is far more prominent in Scripture than the idea of defeat, and apostasy. To the end of time believers have to face indwelling sin, persecution, tribulation and death, yet ultimate triumph is certain and their triumph includes the proclamation of the Gospel on a vast scale to the salvation of an innumerable multitude. Since God uses human instrumentality it goes without saying that nothing will ever be achieved without hard work. Eschatology if it is Biblical, will inspire the fullest use of all our gifts and energies. That view of the future which is all dreams and no action, or which is predominantly defeatist and negative will do no good.

In preparing this bibliography I could not help thinking of a text in Ecclesiastes which reads, 'in the place where the tree falleth, there it shall be'. It seems odd that so many simply follow the eschatological teaching of the seminary in which they trained. Where they went to College – there their views lie. This seems to show that quite a large percentage do not think or read independently. They just fall into one groove like a felled tree. Where the Professor of theology left them, there they lie.

Finally I wonder if there will ever be a great eschatological Conference in which these matters will be sorted out as has been the case with other Biblical issues in the history of the Church?

The books are listed under the different prophetic viewpoints following the same order as Appendix A. Where volumes are currently available the publisher's name is inserted. Details of extent and price (as at June 1968 for books published in England) are included where it is thought that such information might be helpful to the reader. Apart from volumes listed under *The Jews and Israel Today* the bibliography is confined to evangelical authors. Authors are not in alphabetical order. Those books most germane to the subject are listed first.

1. POST-MILLENNIALISM

Commentaries on Romans:

Murray, John.

Marshall, Morgan and Scott. 690 pp. £2.50. Until his retirement in 1967 Professor Murray was professor of Systematic Theology at Westminster Seminary, Philadelphia. His lectures at the Leicester Conference organized by The Banner of Truth have had a profound influence upon many ministers. His two expositions on Romans, chapter 11 at Leicester in July 1964 finally convinced me that the A-millennial interpretation of that chapter is inadequate. It is unlikely that any other commentary on Romans is equal, as far as exegetical thoroughness is concerned, to that of Professor Murray, recently published.

Martyr, Peter.	Commentary published in 1568.
Haldane, Robert.	Banner of Truth. 660 pp. £1.25. More easy to read and less technical than the above-mentioned work. Haldane reasons powerfully for the spiritual restoration of the Jews.
Hodge, Charles.	Eerdmans. 450 pp. For overall usefulness I recommend Hodge on Romans as first. He is excellent on Romans eleven.
Brown, David.	Commentary on Acts and Romans included in commentary on whole Bible by Jamieson, Fausset and Brown. Oliphants. Regarding this work on Romans Spurgeon declared 'Dr. Brown's work must be placed among the first of the first-class. He is a great expositor.'
Parr, Elnathan. (d. 1632?)	1651. A rare and precious old Puritan commentary. Acute insight.
Mason, Archibald.	*Exposition of Romans 11: 25–27.* 1825. A rare book, from which I have derived much inspiration and help.
Moule, H. C. G.	P & I. 437 pp. "The World shall see a spiritual miracle on a scale unknown before. – A transition, relatively swift and wonderful, shall show the world a nation penitent, faithful, holy, given to God."
Allen, Leslie C.	*A New Testament Commentary* Editor G. C. D. Howley "All Israel means the Jews as a collective whole, not the arithmetical sum of all individual Jews." Whatever eschatological views the author may hold elsewhere the sense of his exposition of chapter eleven places him in this company!

Shedd, W. G. T.	Zondervans. A knowledge of Greek required to profit from this work. Shedd shows from the original text that 'all Israel', Rom. 11 : 26, means the Jews.
Barnes, Albert.	Whatever Barnes may teach in other places his commentary on Romans eleven holds firmly to the spiritual restoration of national Israel.
Simeon, Charles.	Vol. 19. Works.

Other works:

Brown, David.	*The Second Advent.* 1849. Reprinted 1953 under the title *Christ's Second Coming.* Also *The Restoration of the Jews 1861.* A valuable book. A weighty scholar and competent commentator, David Brown was champion of the post-millennial interpretation. I have borrowed freely from his work.
Hodge, Charles.	*Systematic Theology,* Vol. 3, pp. 771–868. James Clarke.
Kik, Marcellus. J. 1948.	*Matthew 24.* 115 pp. *Revelation 20,* 1955. 92 pp. Presbyt. and Reformed. Excellent material. Eminently helpful. *Matthew 24* is a classic. It is hardly worth debating the Olivet discourse with folk until they have read Kik! Also important *The Eschatology of Victory.* Craig Press. 1971.
Warfield, B. B.	*Biblical and Theological Studies.* pp. 463–542. Warfield with his giant intellect is in some respects incomparable. Much help has been received from his works and articles. He unfortunately gives the impression in

some places of an earthly Utopia to come.

Edwards, Jonathan. 1703–1758.

The History of Redemption. Sovereign Grace Publishers. 358 pp. This classic work by one of the greatest minds has been sadly neglected. Edwards was no pessimist. Note the following: "Then shall the many nations of Africa, the nations of Negroes, and other heathens who chiefly fill that quarter of the world, who now seem to be in a state but little above the beasts, and in many respects much below them, be enlightened with glorious light, and delivered from all their darkness, and shall become a civil, Christian, understanding, and holy people. Then shall the vast continent of America, which now in so great a part of it is covered with barbarous ignorance and cruelty, be every where covered with glorious gospel light and Christian love; and instead of worshipping the devil, as now they do, they shall serve God, and praises shall be sung every where to the Lord Jesus Christ, the blessed Saviour of the world . . ." p. 314.

Owen, John. 1616–1683.

Works: Goold, Vol. 4, p. 440. Vol. 18, p. 434. Owen declares, "the nation of the Jews, all the world over shall be called, and effectually brought unto the knowledge of the Messiah."

Howe, John 1630–1705.

The Prosperous State of the Christ-Interest Before the End of Time, by a Plentiful Effusion of the Holy Spirit: Considered

153

in Fifteen Sermons on Ezekiel 39:29. "Neither will I hide my face any more from them: for I have poured out my Spirit upon the house of Israel, saith the Lord God." These expositions strengthen one's faith in revival. A salutary reminder of the omnipotence of God!

Boettner, Loraine.
The Millennium. Presbyt. and Reformed. Dr. Boettner is post-millennial but surprisingly does not hold to the spiritual restoration of ethnic Israel. I feel that Dr. Boettner, whose writings are so useful and edifying, has neglected the fact that Romans eleven is the most decisive passage bearing on the subject. He has done much to keep post-millennialism alive during dark days. I owe much to him personally through correspondence.

Bridge, William. 1600–1670.
Works Vol. 4. p. 405. Sermon titled '*Christ's Coming is at our midnight.*' Majestic! Of Christ reigning physically on earth Bridge says, 'I do not see how the saints can spare him out of heaven so long!'

Broughton, Hugh.
Commentary on Daniel, 1596. Broughton is believed to be the first Englishman to offer himself as a herald of the Gospel to the Jews in the Middle East.

Murray, Iain.
The Puritan Hope, 288 pp. Banner of Truth.
A study in Revival and the Interpretation of Prophecy. Excellent from first to last. Particularly helpful is Chapter 9 explaining how all

manner of eschatological error over-
grew the churches during the last
century.

Spurgeon, C. H. Spurgeon preached a sermon titled
*The Restoration and Conversion of the
Jews* on June 16th 1864 at the
Metropolitan Tabernacle (*Metro-
Tab. Pulpit*. Vol. 10. No. 582) in aid
of the funds of the British Society for
the Propagation of the Gospel
amongst the Jews. The text: Ex. 37:
1–10. The headings: 1. There is to
be a political restoration of the Jews,
and Israel is to have a spiritual
restoration or a conversion. 2. The
means of that Restoration. In this
sermon the great Baptist preacher de-
clines 'going into millennial theories,
or into any speculation as to dates.'
But Spurgeon believed that the
Jews would be converted through a
personal appearance of Christ.
Strictly speaking then he was pre-
millennial. However, his Puritanism
caused him to reject cranky prophetic ideas arising during his time.
Quotations could be multiplied from
his sermons to prove that if he were to
choose his company this is where he
would be, and here we gladly welcome him!

Sibbes, Richard. 'There be lesser days before that
1577-1635. great day. As at the first coming of
Christ, so at the overthrow of antichrist, and the conversion of the
Jews, there will be much joy.' Works,
Vol. 2: p. 499, cf. pp. 337, 443, 489,
505: Vol. 5. p. 517.

Finch, Sir Henry.	*The World's Great Restoration, or Calling of the Jews.* Published by William Gouge (1575–1653) 46 years minister at Blackfriars. Gouge was imprisoned by James I in 1621 for publishing the above work, but was released after nine weeks.
Witsius, Hermann. 1636–1708.	*The Conversion of the Jews and the Fulness of the Gentiles,* "their love to him will be the more ardent, as their hatred against him had been formerly more bitter," asserts the author.
Manton, Thomas. 1620–1677.	Works Vol. 14. p. 87. Says Manton, "they are under the care of Providence until they are converted."
Hodge, A. A.	*Outlines of Theology.* p. 568. The author is categorical about the Jews being converted to Christianity as a body.
Snowdon, James H.	*The Coming of the Lord.*
Strong, Augustus.	*Systematic Theology,* 1,160 pp. P & I. £3.00.
Campbell, Roderick.	*Israel and the New Covenant.* Presbyt. and Reformed.
Moore, T. V.	*Commentary on Zechariah.* Banner of Truth. 45p.
Williamson, G. I.	*The Westminster Confession of Faith for Study Classes.* Presbyt. and Reformed. With some additions and a few minor alterations the substance of Appendix A has been taken from this book.
Johnson. E. W.	*The Latter Day Glory.* A most helpful study in manuscript form, 246 pp, by the pastor of Pine Bluff, Arkansas.
Shedd, W. G. T.	*Dogmatic Theology.* 1888, Vol. 2. pp. 591–754.

Fairbairn, Patrick.   *The Interpretation of Prophecy.* 532 pp. Banner of Truth. £1.25. Fairbairn is cautiously post-millennial. He provides material dear to the hearts of those in the A-millennial school.

Kuiper, R. B.   *God Centred Evangelism.* p. 237. Banner of Truth. 30p.

Dabney, Robert L.   *Discussions: Evangelical and Theological*, Vol. 1, p. 210. Banner of Truth. £2.50.

Voetsius, Gisbertus 1589–1676.   *De Generali Conversione Judaeorum* 1636. It is a pity that in their fear of "pietistic elements" so many in the Dutch World of Theology have tended to play down revival as a reality. Voetsius was a true Reformed theologian who believed that the conversion of the Jews would certainly be preceded by a Reformation.

Note:

Of the reformers Martin Bucer, Theodore Beza were post-millennial in their views as were Samuel Rutherford, David Dickson, George Hutcheson, William Perkins, Hugh Broughton, George Gillespie, William Strong and James Durham of the Puritan period. Post-millennialism is expressed in the margins of the Geneva Bible.

2. A-MILLENNIALISM.

Hughes, Archibald.   *The New Heaven and the New Earth.* 1958. Marshall, Morgan and Scott.

Cox, William E.   *A-millennialism Today.* 1966. Presbyt. and Reformed.

Grier, Wm. J.   *The Momentous Event.* 99 pp. 22½p. A

	useful book setting out the different views and providing historical background to them within a brief compass.
Hamilton, Floyd E.	*The Basis of Millennial Faith.*
Kevan, E. F.	Lectures on Eschatology. London Bible College. Having been one of Dr. Kevan's students I record my gratitude for the solid character of his teaching.
Wilmot, John.	*Inspired principles of Prophetic Interpretation.* Foreword by Dr. D. M. Lloyd-Jones. Reiner publications, Swengel, PA. 17880, U.S.A. The purpose of this book is to expose multifarious errors of dispensationalism.
Murray, George L.	*Millennial Studies.*
Lenski, R. C. H.	Commentaries on the New Testament. Augsburg Press. Always militantly A-millennial!
Pieters, Albertus.	*A Candid Examination of the Scofield Bible.* Bible Truth Depot, U.S.A. 27 pp.
Wyngaarden, Martin J.	*The Future of the Kingdom.*
Vos. Geerhardus.	*The Pauline Eschatology.* Eerdmans. 320 pp. First in ability we could well regard Vos as captain of this group!
Hendriksen, William.	*More Than Conquerors.* I.V.F. 280 pp. An exposition of the book of Revelation. *Israel and the Bible.* Baker Book House. 63 pp. See comments p. 40.
Masselink, William.	*Why Thousand Years?*
Hengstenberg, E. W.	*The Revelation.* 2 Volumes.
Allis, Oswald I.	*Prophecy and the Church.* Presbyt. and Reformed. 340 pp. The aim of Dr. Allis throughout is the destruc-

tion of dispensationalism in which he enjoys a large measure of success.

Adams, Jay. *The Time is at Hand*. Pres. & Ref. Pub. Co. 1970. 123 pp. A scholarly, worthwhile book despite its gloom and pessimism which makes Warfield (see Appendices) a real tonic.

Hoeksema, Herman. *Reformed Dogmatics*. Ref. Free. Pub. Ass., U.S.A., 920 pp. Dr. Hoeksema writes at length to prove that 'Israel' in Rom. 11 : 26 means the spiritual and not the ethnic Israel. p. 787. His exposition is much weakened by lack of reference to the terminology used by the apostle throughout the passage to describe ethnic Israel. His remarks only served to confirm my conviction that he was labouring in vain at this point.

Berkhof, Louis. *Systematic Theology*. Banner of Truth. 720 pp. £1.50.

Mauro, Philip. *The Hope of Israel*. Bible Truth Depot, U.S.A. 261 pp. According to Mauro, Israel as a nation has no further role. A swashbuckling onslaught upon dispensationalism.

Van Til, Cornelius. *Christ and the Jews*. 99 pp. Pres. & Ref. Pub. Co. 1968. Suitable only for a microscopic handful absorbed in refuting rationalistic Jewish philosophy.

Note:

Many claim Calvin and Augustine to be A-millennial. Certainly Calvin spiritualizes extensively in A-millennial fashion and in sparse comments on Romans 11 interprets 'all Israel' as 'all the people of God'. It can be truly said that light did not burn brightly on prophetic issues among the Reformers. It should be noted that Augustine foresaw the

THE RESTORATION OF ISRAEL

triumph of Christ's Church. Cf. *The City of God*. And Calvin did not see the course of redemption as a stream which is gradually drying up. He was sustained by his vision of God's plan in history and in his optimism was more like Jonathan Edwards than present day A-millennialists. Although he holds to the spiritual restoration of Israel many would proudly include Dr. Martyn Lloyd Jones in the A-millennial school, as they would Herman Ridderbos and the great Dutch theologian Bavinck. Most Dutch and Afrikaans teachers, including P. A. Verhoof (*Israel in die Krisis*) and W. D. Jonker, follow Ridderbos and are A-millennialists.

3. PRE-MILLENNIALISM

Buswell, J. Oliver.	*Systematic Theology*. Vol. 2 contains a 300-pp. section on eschatology.
Guinness, H. Grattan.	*The approaching end of the age.*
Ladd, George E.	*Crucial Questions about the Kingdom*. 180 pp. *The Blessed Hope*. 160 pp.
Reese, A.	*The Approaching Advent of Christ.*
Sauer, Erich.	*The Dawn of World Redemption. From Eternity to Eternity*. Paternoster.
Frost, H. W.	*The Second Coming.*
Newton, Benjamin Wills	The *Sovereign Grace Advent Testimony* who publish a bi-monthly prophetic
Tregelles, Samuel P.	magazine *Watching and Waiting* have published a few books and a large number of tracts and booklets by Tregelles and Newton. *Prospects of the Ten Kingdoms of the Roman Empire Considered* and *Babylon and Egypt – Their Future and doom* by Newton, and a work on *Daniel* by Tregelles form some of the larger works in this series. Mr. George H. Fromow acts as secretary to S.G.A.T.

Skevington Wood, A.   *Prophecy in the space age.* M.M.&.S. 67½p.

Smith, Oswald J.   *Prophecy – what lies ahead.* M.M.&.S. 62½p.

Poole-Connor, E. J.   *The Coming of the Son of Man.*

Saphir, Adolph.   *The Lord's Prayer.* Contains three chapters on the millennium.

Wilkinson, John.   *Israel my Glory.* 1890. The author was founder of the Mildmay Mission to the Jews.

Hodges, J. W.   *Christ's Kingdom and Coming.* Disappointing. American evangelicals seem bogged down in dispensationalism or in efforts like this one to extricate themselves from the bog. No mention of Romans 11 in 232 pp.!

Note:

Leading exponents during the Puritan period were Thomas Brightman, Joseph Mede, Johann Alsted, Thomas Goodwin, Jeremiah Burroughs (cf. comm. on Hosea). For a detailed study of what some of these men taught see *Puritans, The Millennium and the Future of Israel: Puritan Eschatology 1600 to 1660.* A collection of essays edited by Peter Toon. 157 pp. James Clark.

J. C. Ryle and the Bonar brothers of Scotland, Andrew and Horatius, held the pre-millennial position to which David Baron, Hudson Taylor, George Muller, James Stephens and B. A. Warburton also adhered. Dr. Francis Schaeffer of *L'Abri Foundation*, Switzerland, a foremost Reformed Christian apologist of today is an exponent of this viewpoint as is Ian Tait, well-known minister of *Welwyn Evangelical Church*, Herts, who recommends Ladd's, *The Blessed Hope.*

4. DISPENSATIONALISM

Ryrie, Charles Caldwell.
: *Dispensationalism Today.* Moody Press. Ryrie is an able soldier, fighting for a lost cause.

Chafer, Lewis Sperry.
: *Dispensationalism.* Dallas Seminary Press. Chafer was the founder of Dallas Seminary a stronghold of dispensationalism.

Walvoord, John F.
: *The Return of the Lord.* 160 pp. 92½p. Any-moment pretribulationism!

Bibliotheca Sacra.
: A theological quarterly published by the Dallas Theological Seminary invariably includes a major article defining the principles of interpretation used by dispensationalists. John F. Walvoord is a regular contributor. From 1944–46 an exhaustive study was made of the history of dispensationalist interpretation by Arnold H. Ehlert.

Pentecost, Dwight J.
: *Things to Come.* Denham Pub. Ohio. 633 pp. Pentecost bases much of his teaching on three volumes by George Peters who died in 1909.

McClain, A. J.
: *The Greatness of the Kingdom.* Zandervans, U.S.A.

Olsen, Arnold
: *Inside Jerusalem.* 1968. 240 pp. 30p. Informative but very shallow.

Ironside, H. A.
: *Lectures in Revelation.*

Gray, James M.
: *Prophecy and the Lord's Return.*

Smith, Wilbur M.
: *Israeli Arab Conflict and the Bible.* 1967. 162 pp. (including 44 blank pages!) 30p. Interesting chapters on the territorial restoration of Israel and Arab enmity. The part on Jerusalem's future is unsatisfactory – a jumble of uncollated quotations

	based on unproved dispensational assumptions. Romans 11 is left out in the cold.
Wolff, Richard.	*Israel Act 3*. 1967. 94 pp. 30p. Thin, disorderly, and inconclusive!
Scofield, C. I.	*The Scofield Reference Bible*. A new revised edition published in 1967. Among the editors are several well-known evangelicals such as Wilbur Smith, John F. Walvoord, F. E. Gaebelein, William Culbertson, Allan A. Macrae and Alva J. McClain.
Darby, J. N.	Darby was one of the fathers of Dispensationalism. His prophetic views colour most of his writings. The same is true of other 'brethren' writers such as C. H. Mackintosh.
Gromacki, R. G.	*Are These the Last Days?* 190 pp. Henry E. Walter. Here in crimson are all the man tenets of dispensationalism fervently set forth. Buy this and you will need no other to represent this section.

Note:

Wilbur Smith in his bibliography to *Israel Arab Conflict* draws attention to the fact that there is a great mass of important material relating to the interpretation of the prophetic Scriptures in hundreds of articles appearing in the then widely-read prophetic journals of a century ago, such as *Journal of Prophecy*, 1849–1858; *The Investigator*, London, 1831–1836; *The Jewish Expositor and Friend of Israel*, London, 1816–1834; *Prophetic News*, 1877– 00; *The Morning Watch*, Edinburgh, 1888–1895; and other periodicals.

THE JEWS AND ISRAEL TODAY.

The following titles are selected from a wide range of books. The large number of secular volumes on sale today reflects the interest that prevails in this subject.

Historical

Roth, Cecil.

Short History of the Jewish People (East and West. Lib. 1953). *The World History of the Jewish People*. Vol. II. The Dark Ages. W. H. Allen. 1,000 pp. £5.25. Under the supervision of Prof. Roth this is the first volume of what looks like a very ambitious project. David Ben-Gurion has given his blessing to the work. He makes the remark, 'There is no "Palestine" in the world – it exists only in our enemies' aspirations to destroy us.' We are to call the land *Israel*. Other authors on the history of the Jews are: Goodman, Grayzel and Graetz, the latter in six vols.

Max Wurmbrand and Cecil Roth.

The Jewish People – 4,000 Years of Survival. Thames and Hudson. 462 pp. £5.25. Beautifully illustrated. An ideal introduction to Jewish history.

James, E. O.

Jerusalem – A History. Hamlyn 294 pp. £6.30. A large size volume, magnificently illustrated especially for those who appreciate art and architecture. Deficient nevertheless in information and maps.

Parke, James.

A History of the Jewish People. Penguin. 22½p. A bit dry.

Dimont, Max. I.

Jews, God and History. A popular paperback. Readable and informative.

Ausebel, Nathan.   *Pictorial History of the Jewish People.* 426 pp. Crown Pub. New York. A popular work. Ideal as an introduction to the subject.

Reitlinger, G.   *The Final Solution.* Vallentine Mitchell. 620 pp. Regarded as the standard work documenting Nazi extermination of the Jews. Other authors covering the subject are Arthur D. Morse, *When Six Million Died*, and Yuri Suhl, *They Fought Back*. All these and Horbach's *Out of the Night* were reviewed in *The Times Saturday Review*, April 20 1968. The present weekly series *History of the Second World War* ($17\frac{1}{2}$p per issue) provides valuable information. Rudolf Vrba, a Czechoslovakian Jew, who escaped from Auschwitz, has contributed a short but gripping article included in Vol. 5. No. 13.

Dawidowitz, Lucy S.   *The Golden Tradition.* Edited by Lucy S. Dawidowitz. Vallentine Mitchell. 502 pp. £2.75. For more than five hundred years, until the holocaust of 1940–1945, Eastern Europe was the centre of the Jewish world. Large numbers emigrated to America and Israel. The broad social, political and historical background to East European Jewry is painted in a variety of colours, the brush strokes consisting of biographical sketches, essays and quotations from leading East European Jews of the past. A copious source of well-edited and interesting material most of which reflects the hopelessness of Jewry

165

without the Lord Jesus. It makes one cry out, 'Oh, when will they believe?'

Antonius, George. *The Arab Awakening*. Hamish Hamilton. 455 pp. A valuable history of the Arab movement from 1847–1935.

Sokolov, Nahum. *History of Zionism*. 2 vols. Regarded as the standard work.

Borchenius, Paul. *And it was Morning*. 218 pp. Allen and Unwin. £1.40. The author, a Danish pastor, has written five volumes describing various eras of Jewish history of which the above is the most interesting. A moving account of the Final Solution is included. A well-written work translated from the Danish.

Lipman, V. D. *Social History of the Jews in England 1850–1950*. Watts and Co. 200 pp.

Peretz, D. *Israel and the Palestine Arabs*.

Friedmann, Georges. *The End of the Jewish People* Hutchinson. 300 pp. Translated from the French by Eric Mosbacher. £2.25. A pessimistic but superb book nevertheless. Friedman was a nominal Jew until the Nazis occupied France in 1940. Subsequent post-war visits to Israel have stirred him, like many others, to the depths. He is particularly helpful in dealing with problems such as: resisting the menace of mass culture, the population structure of Israel, and the religious problem in which he calls for prophets in the place of rabbis. Jewish aspirations of messianic mission to the Third World is described. In this respect it is interesting to note that Dr. Hastings Banda, president of Malawi, supports Israel largely because of his Christian convictions and careful reading of the Bible. His positive statements on the subject were reported in *The Times*, June 12, 1968.

Prittie, Terence. *Israel – Miracle in the Desert.* Pall Mall. 246 pp. £2.25.

Bermant, Chaim. *Israel.* Thames and Hudson. 224 pp. £1.75. Written after the Six-day war. A fine all-round description of the country.

Houghton, S. M. *Tourist in Israel.* Banner of Truth. 224 pp. 25p. Written just prior to the Six-day war. Interesting chapter on Masada.

Churchill, Randolph and Winston S. *The Six-day War.* Heineman. 250 pp. Regarded by many as the best short account of the war.

Eisenstadt, S. N. *Israel Society.* Weidenfeld and Nicolson. 450 pp. £3.75.

Ami Ben. *Between Hammer and Sickle.* Jew. Pub. Soc. of America. 300 pp. This book describes the situation of Jews in Russia today. Reports are documented that the Communists allow some churches and synagogues to function merely as showpieces to deceive naïve visitors from the West.

Douglas-Home, Charles. *The Arabs and Israel.* 1968. The Bodley Head. 75p.

Sykes, Christopher. *Cross Roads to Israel.* Collins. 479 pp. £2.10.

Ben-Gurion, David. *Israel, Years of Challenge.* Anthony Blond. 240 pp. Vigorous, clear writing by a great politician, a man of extraordinary determination and courage.

Edelman, Maurice. *Ben Gurion*, a political biography. Hodder and Stoughton. 206 pp. £1.50.

Lau-Lavie, Napthali. *Moshe Dayan*, a biography. Vallentine Mitchell. 222 pp. £1.50. Highly readable. A simple way to become acquainted with modern history of Israel is to view it through the eye of this famous soldier whose story is well told by Lau-Lavie.

Nassbaum, Elizabeth. *Israel*. Oxford University Press. 127 pp. 42½p. Well worth the price.

Abrahams, Gerald. *The Jewish Mind*. Constable. 400 pp. £1.75. Setting out to discuss 'what is a Jew?' – the writer wanders all over the place occasionally providing interesting insights.

Comay, Joan. *Introducing Israel*. Methuen. 302 pp. A comprehensive and informative account of Israel and her people.

Conway, J. S. *The Nazi Persecution of the Churches 1933–1945.* Weidenfeld and Nicolson. 474 pp. £6.25. Immense research lies behind this fascinating book, 135 pp. of which consists of documentary material. The author shows:
1. That sweeping statements are to be shunned in regard to anti-semitism in the churches.
2. That ultimately Nazism was determined to crush Christianity in every shape and form.
3. That Nazism ought always to remind us to avoid naïve attitudes in respect of anti-democratic forces.

Bentwich, Norman. *Israel – Two fateful Years 1967–69.* Elek. 115 pp. £1.25. Judicious,

	sensitive and fair, especially in regard to Arab-Israeli relationships. Warmly commended.
Fast, Howard.	*The Jews*. Cassel. 338 pp. £3.15. A racey history marred by the worst possible caricature of Paul and his teaching. cf. pp. 121 ff.

WHO IS A CHRISTIAN?

From the religious standpoint there is no more important question than this – who is a Christian? The New Testament is surely the only basis upon which we can establish a satisfactory and authoritative definition. In turning to the Gospels and epistles we are left in no doubt whatever as to who constitutes a Christian. The following factors can be deemed essential requirements:

1. The Christian believes that Jesus Christ is the Son of God, equal with the Father, and the only Saviour. By faith in Christ the Christian is assured of forgiveness of sin and reconciliation to the Father who declares him to be just.

2. The Christian is one who has been born again of the Holy Spirit. He has been the subject of a complete and radical change or conversion, in which every aspect of life has become new. The Old and New Testaments have become the only authoritative basis for doctrine and ethics. This inward renewal, a new nature, results in the fruits of the Spirit which are love, joy, peace, long-suffering, gentleness and meekness. It follows that anyone who maliciously persecutes Jews, or any other nation for that matter, is immediately disqualified and cannot be a true Christian. This does not spell pacifism, for it is a man's duty to protect life or country from aggressors, but it does mean compassion, humility, sincerity and constancy in aiming at peace with all men.

3. The Christian is one who by the Holy Spirit has an intimate knowledge of the Father and of Jesus Christ, which spiritual life is maintained by regular reading of the Old and New Testaments, and by prayer.

Since the time of Jesus Christ Christians have been a small minority in society. It is doubtful whether their number has, at any point in history, ever exceeded the equivalent number of Jews in the world.

Up to the time of the reformation Christians were 'Ecclesiola in Ecclesia' 'a church within the Church'. In other words, true, faithful, practising Christians formed a small segment working within the overall structure. In the Holy Roman Empire the Church and society were regarded as one entity. There was very little about this Empire that deserved the title of 'holy'. Some of the Popes were the epitome of wickedness. Nevertheless the Papacy assumed authority over all so-called Christian countries to form 'The Church'.[1]

The reformation proved to be the mightiest movement since the days of Pentecost. The truth which had been buried by a massive, predominantly secular system was unearthed once more. Gospel light shone brightly. The definition of 'Who is a Christian' just propounded is in full accord with the teaching of the Reformers of the 16th century, the Puritans of the 17th, the revivalist leaders of the 18th, and the illustrious missionaries such as Carey and Livingstone of the last century. While clarity pertained at the time of the Reformation in regard to the nature of a Christian, this was not the case with the nature of the church. Whole States simply became Protestant. The old error of regarding Church and State as one, was perpetuated. There were, however, smaller groups who rightly claimed that the Church should consist exclusively of those who show genuine spiritual life, and that Church and State should be separate. This concept, which is Biblical, has spread widely and today gathered churches of Bible believing Christians are to be found all over the world. Each local church must be judged on its merits. It is important for Jews to understand that the church is not a whole country or ethnic group but rather the gathering of the spiritual out of the world for the true worship of God.

Society is Christian in name only. The true Christians are

---

1. The very word Church, *Ek-Klesia*, means 'called out of', inferring a body of people called out of the world. To ascribe the word 'Church' to the world as a whole is a misnomer. For instance, we have Roman Catholic Spain, Anglican England, Greek Orthodox Greece or Lutheran Scandinavia. In each case it is misleading to think of nations as churches.

drawn out of society to form the Church. Thus it is folly to assert that Nazi Germany was Christian. It is doubtful whether there were one in a hundred who believed on Jesus Christ in the apostolic sense in Germany in 1939, just as in Britain today it is possible to visit a hundred homes before coming to one where the Bible is ever opened, let alone read, believed and practised. Visiting several thousand homes in this particular area (where there is probably a higher percentage of Christians than in most other parts of Britain) I estimate that about 2 per cent of the population publicly confess Jesus Christ as Lord and Saviour, keep the Lord's Day as a holy day, and maintain a life of prayer, witness and spirituality. Of these there are generally speaking about twice as many non-conformist believers (Brethren, Baptist, Congregational etc.,) as Church of England believers. As far as anti-semitism is concerned among these, who are commonly known as evangelicals, I have never come across so much as a trace of it.

We all do well then, to be more careful in the use of the word 'Christian'. The great Ecumenical movement of our day is ominous because it represents nominal Christianity. Such bodies always tend to persecute. The most bloody persecutions of history emanate from unspiritual bodies purporting to be spiritual when they are not. It was so from the beginning. Joseph was spiritual, but his brothers hated him, persecuted him and would have murdered him, but for the intervention of Reuben. They sold him to Egypt instead. And then, in the case of the great prophet Moses, far from gaining the loyal support of Israel, the majority proved to be unspiritual and rebellious. It took forty years in the wilderness to attain enough discipline to enter the promised land. The history which followed is hardly one of unity. Many of the foremost prophets, such as Elijah, complained of loneliness. The majority of people maintained an outward profession only and disliked the searching preaching of the prophets.

If we are to define a Christian let us be consistent and allow the Bible to delineate his features. Let the guilt of anti-semitism be laid where it belongs – at the door of nominal secular Christianity – and especially Rome. Rev: 17:6.

Writing in the *Daily Telegraph* Supplement[1] David Pryce Jones declared recently:

> 'The compliance of the European clergy in the destruction of Jewry, grown men like Cardinal Faulheber and Cardinal Seredi down to parish priests, is no longer in doubt. Auschwitz for a leading German Theologian is "Christianity's greatest defeat".
>
> 'On Good Friday, 1959, Pope John XXIII took the decision to purge the Roman Catholic liturgy of its anti-semitic language. It was a momentous step. Since the Second Vatican Council Catholics are no more to pray for help against *perfidia*; *judaica*, the Jewish perfidy.'

When I refer, therefore, in this book to *Christians* or *Christianity* or to *New Testament Christianity* I mean by that, evangelical, spiritual, Christianity. I am not referring to national cultures or to those ugly monolithic structures which falsely assume the name of Christian, who may use Christ's name, but who do not fulfil his precepts. And when I refer to *Hebrew Christians* I mean those who are Jewish by blood and who follow the steps of the apostles. From what we can gather all the apostles were of Hebrew stock.

---

1. David Pryce Jones, *Daily Telegraph Magazine.* 22 January 1971.

WHO IS A JEW?

No controversy vexes the land of Israel more than this question. It is being debated at every level, including the Knesset (Israeli Parliament). As in the case of a Christian there is ultimately only one valid basis for definition as to who is a Jew. That is the Bible. The name itself is derived from Judah, one of the twelve sons of Jacob, after whom the Southern Kingdom, with Jerusalem as the capital, was named. After the death of Solomon the nation divided and the Northern Kingdom became known as Israel which was the name given to Jacob after his spiritual ordeal at Peniel. Gen 32:38. From a physical point of view all descendants of Abraham, through Isaac, are Jewish whether of the line of Israel or Judah. In any case, the Northern Kingdom (Israel) was dispersed at the time of Assyrian invasion in 722 B.C. It is now almost impossible for Jews to trace back their lineage to so early a date.

What percentage of blood is necessary to qualify as a descendant? The rule which has applied in present day Israel, until recently, was that a Jewish mother is essential. The apostle Paul, himself a Jew of the highest order, of the tribe of Benjamin, raised the matter to a spiritual level by saying that we ought to discern between spiritual Jews and merely nominal Jews, that is the physical descendants of Abraham, through Isaac. 'For he is not a Jew, which is one outwardly; neither is that circumcision, which is outward in the flesh: But he is a Jew, which is one inwardly; and circumcision is that of the heart, in the spirit, and not in the letter; whose praise is not of men, but of God.' Rom. 2:28,29.

A common error made by Jews has been to rest in the carnal security of possessing status, merely because of physical descent. Hence John the Baptist, the promised forerunner of the Messiah, reproved the Jews of his day by declaring; 'Say not to yourselves, we have Abraham to our father: for I say unto you, that God is able of these stones to raise up children unto Abraham.' Matt. 3:9.

Some take this as a veiled reference to the calling of the Gentile nations from whom God was soon to raise up a multitude who would love and serve him in truth. Thus, many Old Testament prophecies concerning the calling of the Gentiles on a universal scale would find fulfilment. Is. 42:6, 66:12.

Most references to the Jews (Yehudim) made in the Old Testament are to be found in the book of Esther, but frequently also in Jeremiah, Nehemiah and Ezra. In Babylon, the word Jew in the strict sense signified someone of Judah. Almost every reference (and there are about two hundred) in the New Testament refer to the Jews in a general sense whether they lived in the South, the North or abroad. The terms 'children of Israel' and 'sons of Jacob' are often used in the Old Testament to describe the Jews.

Turning to the question in the contemporary context, the religious ruling, in Israel, as has been said, is that Jewish descent follows from the mother, providing she has not adopted another faith. Those officially converted to Judaism who may have no Jewish descent are also included. Any Jew living in any country whatsoever is welcome to return to his homeland where he will automatically qualify for Israeli citizenship. But, as is to be expected, there are exceptional and intricate cases which have proved very controversial.

The instance can be cited of a Soviet mixed marriage, the father being a Jew but the mother a non-Jewish Russian girl.[1] In Russia the family are regarded as Jewish but not in Israel. In order to qualify the non-Jewish mother must undergo religious instruction, examinations and conversion. Opinions differ as to how long this process should last. Some Israelis are very angry that something like this should be allowed to discourage immigration.

The rule about the mother being Jewish was broken during

---

1. Most Soviet Jews arriving in Israel are complete Jewish families unaffected by inter-marriage, and that despite a long period of anti-religious propaganda in Russia. *The Daily Telegraph*. 24 February 1971.

1970 when a major in the Israeli army succeeded in obtaining a ruling that his two children be registered as Jews by nationality, despite the fact that his Gentile wife had not been converted to Judaism. But now a law has been passed to the effect that Jewishness will be determined according to religious law with an endorsement that Jewishness derives from the mother. Thus the religious and ethnic principles combine, being incorporated into civil law.

Maier Asher writing for the *Daily Telegraph* from Jerusalem[1] describes the furore which followed this decision, referring to the drama enacted in front of the Knessett when Hanan Frank, an immigrant from Holland, who lost both his legs in a battle against Arab terrorists, shouted, 'Nobody doubted I was a Jew when I went into action, not even the Arabs!' The fact is that Hanan Frank's father is a Jew but not his mother, which, according to the letter of the law, deprives him of his nationality.

Jews, generally speaking, like nominal Christians, are ignorant of the Scriptures. If they would read both Testaments they would find that male descent, that is descent from the father, is always of first importance. Thus, while Jesus derived his humanity from his mother alone, the Holy Spirit is scrupulous to provide the complete genealogy of Joseph, his legal guardian.

In Israel Chief Rabbi Untermann has asserted that, 'intermarriage is the kiss of death for the Jewish nation'. Evangelical Christians believe the same knowing that the spiritual life of a believer is crippled if united to an unbeliever. II Cor. 6: 14–18.

The history of the Jews is fascinating. That this race has survived a dispersion into all nations as well as the most horrible persecution is amazing. Is not this the finger of God? The amazing history of the Hebrews serves to make their present situation even more interesting. They have been preserved intact. That some are of impure descent is inevitable and we can be sure that the controversy, 'Who is a Jew?', will continue. The origins are recorded in the Bible and to that source alone one should turn for light and clarity.

---

1. ibid.

APPENDIX F.

WHAT ABOUT THE FALLING AWAY?

There has probably been more misconception about the 'falling away' than any other aspect in regard to eschatology. Most of this arises out of misunderstanding the 20th chapter of Revelation. Hundreds of books have been written on the Apocalypse and hardly two agree on details since the book is essentially symbolic in character. Once we start to literalize the symbolic where do we end?

B. B. Warfield in an article on 'The Second Coming'[1] has a moving description of the conquering church described in the 19th chapter in which he shows that the purpose of John the Apostle is to picture both the Church safely gathered above together with the militant struggling Church here below. 'Not the one alone, but both together pass unscathed through the great trial (latter part of Chapter 20) to inherit the new heavens and the new earth. (Chapter 21). John is here only saying in symbols what Paul says in more direct language when he tells us that, whether we wake or sleep, we shall all live together with our Lord Jesus Christ in that great day when death is swallowed in victory. (1 Thess. 4 : 15; v : 10; 1 Cor. 15 : 39ff).''

Some may well object that this is to pass over too quickly the 7th verse, 'and when the thousand years are expired Satan shall be loosed out of his prison and shall go out to deceive the nations which are in the four quarters of the earth'. We should be very cautious in coming to any definite conclusions about the future, from the Book of Revelation, whereas the plain statements of Paul, which are not apocalyptic or symbolic, furnish us with materials for an absolutely clear grasp of future events.

If we are to insist on details from Rev. 20:7, then, to be consistent, we should note that Satan's activities must to a large

---

1. This article is to be found in his *Selected Shorter Writings* edited by J. E. Meeter cf. pp. 348. Pres. & Ref. Pub. Co. 1970.

extent be curtailed in the four quarters of the earth. This presupposes an effectual spreading of the Gospel on a vast scale which in turn implies that if there is to be a falling away then there must be something from which to fall. Warfield did not believe in a falling away at the end. He takes the two symbols 'a thousand years' and 'a little time' as a contrast: The heavenly bliss as against the earthly turmoil and evil. Exteriority, not subsequence, is suggested. That is, those who are not yet with Christ in Paradise have yet to endure a little season of Satan's buffetings.[1]

The thousand years taken symbolically represents the whole dispensation of Christ's reign from the time of his ascension and exaltation to the time of his coming again. The terms 'premillennial' and 'postmillennial', in that they imply a thousand year period, are misleading terms, even though they may be useful to describe the different prophetic viewpoints.

The Man of Sin. 2 Thess. 2:1-12.

Some have seen a falling away spelled out in the terms employed by the apostle in his 2nd Epistle to the Thessalonians. This apostasy is to take place before the coming again of Christ to end the world and to usher in the great judgment. A lawless one (v. 8) would be revealed. The appearing of that wicked one would take place when a restraining power would be removed. Warfield shows in his usual thorough way that Paul was referring to contemporary events. The destruction of Jerusalem had not yet taken place at the time of Paul's writing.[2] We now have no adequate conception of the malice let loose upon the Christians in the ten successive persecutions following the removal of Judaism which Warfield takes to be the restraining power. Caligula, Nero, Vespasian and Domitian, he describes as 'those hideous ganglia' who vent their wrath upon the Christians. The separation of Christianity from Juda-

---

1. Article, *The Millennium and the Apocalypse*; reprinted in *Biblical Doctrines*, pp. 649-651.
2. *Biblical and Theological Studies*. Pres. & Ref. Pub. Co. p. 463 ff.

ism removed a protective screen and gave the signal for the lawless one to shower his horrible rage upon the churches.

As for the description in 2 Thess. 2:4 of the Man of Sin 'sitting in the temple of God, showing that he is God,' Warfield takes this to be a reference to Matt. 24:15 described by our Lord as 'the abomination of desolation which was spoken of by Daniel the Prophet standing in the Holy place.''[1] Christopher Wordsworth,[2] one time Canon of Westminster, believed (as did not a few of the Reformers) that 2 Thess. 2:4 refers to the Pope and the Papacy. This is interesting but Warfield's exposition seems more compelling. It should be noted, however, that from the time of Constantine onwards a falling away from Apostolic Christianity of landslide proportions took place. This may well be the fulfilment of II Thess. 2:3.

Antichrist

References to 'antichrist' are found exclusively in the epistles of John (1 John 2:18, 22; 4:3, 2 John 7). It would seem that many of his readers were oppressed in their imaginations with the dread anticipation of the coming of antichrist, which situation the apostle handles by asserting that the coming of antichrist had already taken place. The phenomenon was not something to be looked forward to with uncertainty, but rather something which had to be faced with courage in everyday life. John makes it quite clear that we are already living in 'the last hour' by which he means the Messianic period, being the total time from the first coming of the Messiah until the second appearing. (1 John 2:18 cf. The phraseology of the N.T. I Pet. 1:20, Heb 1:2, James 5:3, II Tim. 3:1.) There can be no question that the Apostle John removes the idea of an individual antichrist and substitutes him for a multitude of antichrists which embody the spirit of antichrist. And in 1 John 4:3, we can hardly imagine that the Apostle is speaking of an individual antichrist since he is telling his readers how to recognize antichrist spirits.

---

1. *Biblical and Theological Studies*. Pres. & Ref. Pub. Co. p. 472.
2. *Babylon: The Church of Rome*, p. 67.

Certainly these seducing spirits emanate from Satan, who is the epitome of all that is antichrist (2 John 7). To quote Warfield again, 'So long as a divine Christ is confessed in the midst of a gainsaying world, so long will there be many antichrists.'[1]

Conclusion

After close examination of the passages which seem to point to a falling away and the revelation of an antichrist one must conclude that a great deal of imagination has been employed in adding detail to these passages. False ideas form easily which afterwards become very difficult to eradicate. We do well to remember that both in 2 Thess. 2 and the epistles of John the purpose of the writers was to circumvent baleful conclusions rather than encourage them.

---

1. Cf. *Selected Shorter Writings* of B. B. Warfield edited by J. E. Meeter p. 356.

APPENDIX G.

THE IMMINENCY OF CHRIST'S RETURN

Many Christians cannot understand how expectation of further ingatherings of souls, which may take many years, can be compatible with the text found in Peter's second epistle, 'Looking for and hasting unto the coming of the day of the Lord', II Peter 3:12.

In support of the view that believers should expect that any moment the Lord might return, Titus 2:13 is also quoted: 'Looking for that blessed hope and the glorious appearing of the great God and our Saviour Jesus Christ'. The exhortation of Paul to the Thessalonians, 'to wait for his son from heaven', which is repeated in a slightly different form to the Corinthians (I Cor. 1:7) is quoted as a further example as is Phil. 3:20, 'our citizenship is in heaven; from whence also we wait for a Saviour'. (R.V.)

The Thessalonian Christians would seem to have inferred that the return of Christ was expected during their lifetime, which misconception is corrected in the second letter. Here they are informed that certain events would have to take place before the second advent of the Saviour. Some Thessalonians had misconstrued Paul's first letter, to the extent of giving up secular work. What point in labouring if the world was soon to end? Paul reminded them of the basic principle that not to work is not to eat. There is no room for sloth. But, to return to the subject, two specific aspects must find fulfilment before Christ returns. First there must be a falling away and secondly the man of sin must be revealed.

From this it must be conceded that not only those who believe in the spiritual restoration of Israel face a difficult problem, but also those who believe that a falling away and the revelation of a man of sin are yet to come. As shown elsewhere in these pages, there are those who hold that both these events have already transpired. Yet the imminency of Christ's return is affected by the fact that we await the ingathering of the Jews and great awakenings among the Gentile nations.

Although some will find it very hard to accept, we have here an *antinomy*. The Shorter Oxford Dictionary defines an antinomy as 'a contradiction between conclusions which seem equally logical, reasonable or necessary'. It would be better to say an antinomy represents an *appearance* of contradiction, for the main point is that there is no real contradiction at all, although it looks like one. An *apparent* incompatibility exists between two clearly defined truths.

Thus, we have the antinomy of human responsibility and absolute predestination. We might very well end up as Pelagians if we hold only to human responsibility, or as hyper-Calvinists if we hold only to absolute predestination. Both are equally important, even though they will never simultaneously be reconciled to human reason.

Thus, it is a plain fact that we are to believe in the imminency of Christ's coming yet, at the same time, know that much has to happen before that great consummating event.

For instance, we can cite the case of Enoch who prophesied of the imminent coming of the Lord, Jude v. 14. It is interesting to observe the word *cometh*, *ēlthe* literally means 'is come', that is, He shall and certainly will come as if He were come already. In other words, Enoch was preaching the imminency of Christ's return and that 'with ten thousands of His saints'. As in the book of Revelation, we interpret the ten thousand as a symbol of round and high reckoning. Christ is coming with colossal multitudes of angels and saints. But how could Christ's second coming be imminent when He had not even come the first time? This points us to the answer.

Every generation is to look to the great day which is, at one and the same time, the great appearing of Jesus Christ; the great judgment day; the end of the world; the inauguration of the new heavens and the new earth. At this time, those who have died will be joined with their bodies in a state of glorification. Those who are alive at the Lord's coming will be changed in an instant and taken up to meet Him in the air.

Tremendous ethical implications are involved. The Judgment which occurs when Christ is revealed will be of the most meticulous order. We are to associate the final judgment with the second coming. Then it is that our final and eternal state will be settled. For these reasons we are all to look to the heavens from whence our Saviour will come. To the Lord a thousand years is as a day. By this reckoning Enoch prophesied only last week and certainly by next week Christ will have returned.

Thus while some may find an obstacle in this teaching we should remember that this has not been so with believers who hold to the position that has been outlined.

About forty generations have passed since the Ascension of Christ. Throughout this period believers have been looking for His coming. Those who die go directly to be with the Lord where they join us in looking for that Great Day. In other words, their expectation is the same as ours, and this is what Paul is trying to teach the Thessalonians. Apart from the fact that they will escape the pain of death, there is no great material advantage to those who are alive at the Lord's coming.

In conclusion, let it be said that it is quite compatible to exhort people to look for and wait for the coming of the Lord and at the same time to teach them to pray for revival which naturally they would expect to see before the Lord's appearing.

APPENDIX H.

THE RECOVERY OF POSTMILLENNIALISM

In 1961 the dispensationalist leader, J. Vernon McGhee, stated that Postmillennialism was dead and that no American theologian held to it. This was not entirely accurate since Loraine Boettner's work, *The Millennium*, appeared in 1957. Editions of Loraine Boettner's book have appeared every three years. Boettner does not himself believe in any major Jewish conversion in the future. In this respect he differs from the theologian he most admires, namely, B. B. Warfield, who has been recognized as the outstanding Postmillennial theologian. Warfield died in 1921. His works have been reprinted spasmodically. One would think that his brilliant mind and luminous style would have wide appeal. This, however, is not the case, the simple reason being that the majority prefer material which does not require the concentration of the order required by Warfield, who has been compared with Calvin for his power to penetrate Biblical subjects. As we would expect, B. B. Warfield spotted the crucial point in regard to the restoration of Israel, namely that everything hinges on the interpretation of the two words, 'All Israel'.[1] The 'All Israel' he took to mean the fleshly or ethnic Israel, which calling would be followed in turn by 'the widest practicable extension of Christianity'.

But to return to Postmillennialism today, as far as I know, this study, *The Restoration of Israel*, has been alone in the field as far as available books are concerned, both in regard to the ground it covers and the position it takes. Naturally, books which are available today in shops and easily accessible to the Christian public carry far more weight than books which are only to be found in libraries, even though the books in the libraries may be more worthy than the present day available

---

1. *Biblical and Theological Studies*, p. 486. Pres. & Ref. Pub. Co.

ones! Iain Murray's book, *The Puritan Hope* (1971), follows the same interpretation as has been taken in this book, and provides abundant proof from history that this 'Cinderella' is the true princess and heiress of the Reformed Faith. Mr Murray's book is particularly valuable in providing information on the history of eschatology during the last century showing how the old Postmillennialism has been displaced by other views, particularly by dispensationalism emanating from people like J. N. Darby.

Through correspondence it has become clear to me that there is a rennaissance of faith in the old Postmillennial viewpoint. Moreover, much work has been attempted which has not been published, it being no easy matter to persuade publishers to produce material which does not have a wide appeal. This situation is gradually changing. For instance one of the unpublished manuscripts is by E. W. Johnson.[1] He makes headway in expounding some of the Old Testament prophets. Since there are numerous passages which seem to indicate a tremendous ingathering of Gentiles (such as we have not yet seen) we do well to endeavour to collate these passages and to interpret them carefully. Nor can they be dismissed by simply asserting that they belong to the Old Testament. Reformed theology has taught us to regard the Word of God as a unity.

It is hoped that in the future greater progress will be made than ever before in the exposition of both Old and New Testament Scriptures and the writer is confident that the Postmillennial position will go from strength to strength. The renewal of hope should draw evangelicals out of their blinkers of negative, pessimistic defeatism, to storm the gates of hell once more. May it please God to make it so.

---

1. Johnson deals briefly with the prophecies of Moses, Isaiah, Ezekiel, Daniel, Micah, Habakkuh, Zechariah and Malachi. Needless to say that attention needs to be devoted to the Psalms, Hosea and Joel as well as other parts of the Old Testament not mentioned here.

APPENDIX I.

TO ZION OR OUT OF ZION?

The apostle Paul's use of prepositions and the way in which he quotes the Old Testament in regard to *Zion* (see p. 59) deserves special attention.

'As it is written the Deliverer will come out of Zion and turn ungodliness away from Jacob.' (Rom. 11:26.) The apostle quotes Isaiah 59:20, which reads, 'and the Deliverer shall come *to* Zion, and unto them that turn from transgression in Jacob'. In the most literal and exact way the Messiah fulfilled the prophecy of Isaiah. He came to Zion and the remnant who turned from transgression recognized him as their sin-bearer and Saviour.

But Paul looks further than this fulfilment. He sees a mercy reserved for the future. God having connected a blessing with Abraham in perpetuity could not rescind it, 'for the gifts and calling of God are without repentance'. There would always be some who would believe but besides this, there was reserved 'a fulness'. If all the families in the earth are to be blessed in Abraham and a fulness accrue in respect of them, how much more the family from which the blessing originally sprang?

The old literal Zion with all its externalities is now gone. The new Zion in which the Redeemer now lives has been established. Out of this heavenly Jerusalem, the New Testament Church, the Redeemer will come to turn ungodliness away from those in Jacob. Thus, the mercy received by the Gentiles is to be the reflux by which the natural Israel is to be called.

It is not a literal re-establishment of the old structure that we look for. That has been abrogated for ever. The New Testament Church is the Zion inhabited by Christ. He cannot come to that Zion for he already dwells in her. But his gracious presence is to be manifested from out of her, and by her instrumentally ungodliness in Jacob is to receive its death wound. Joel 3:21.

Therefore, to use the words of Patrick Fairbairn, 'Let the Church that already dwells with Him in this Zion (Heb. 12:22) go forth in His name, and deal in faith and love with these descendents of the natural Israel. – – let her do it *now*, not waiting for things that, if they shall ever happen, lie beyond the limits alike of her responsibility and her control".[1]

---

1. *The Typology of Scriptures.* Vol. 1. p. 390.ff.

APPENDIX J.

TEXTUAL INDEX

IMPORTANT DATES IN THE HISTORY OF ISRAEL[1]

B.C.	1921	The call of Abraham and the birth of the Jewish people.
	1897	Isaac is born.
	1853	Jacob and Esau are born.
	1729	Joseph is carried as a slave into Egypt.
	1706	Jacob and his sons join Joseph in Egypt.
	1689	Jacob's death. He prophesies that the messiah will come from Judah.
	1571	Moses is born.
	1491	Moses leads the children of Israel out of Egypt.
	1451	Joshua makes conquest of Canaan.
	1030	Saul becomes the first king of Israel.
	1011	David becomes king.
	972	Solomon begins his reign.
	933	The land is divided into two kingdoms.
	721	The Northern Kingdom is taken by the Assyrians.
	587	The Southern Kingdom falls to Nebuchadnezzar of Babylon.
	538 – 515	Return from Babylonian captivity.
	457 – 424	Ezra and Nehemiah.
	333	Alexander makes conquest of Palestine.
	63	Beginning of Roman rule.
	5	Birth of Jesus.
A.D.	28	Crucifixion of Jesus.
	70	Jerusalem destroyed.
	73	Fall of Masada.
	132 – 135	Revolt of Bar Kochba.
	637	Beginning of Arab rule in Palestine.
	1099–1291	Crusader period.
	1291–1561	Muslim period.
	1799	Napoleon defeated in Palestine.
	1917	Allenby enters Jerusalem. Britain becomes custodian of Palestine. The Balfour declaration.
	1933–1945	The Hitler régime and holocaust.
	1948	British mandate ends. Proclamation of the State of Israel.
	1948–1949	War with the Arabs.
	1950	Law of return, confirming right of every Jew to live in Israel.
	1956	Israeli forces occupy Sinai peninsula.
	1967	Six-day war in which Israel defeats Egypt, Jordan and Syria.

---

1. n.b. Historians differ in their estimates of early dates particularly those preceding 1,000 B.C.